D0992637

"This book is funny, insightful, informational, wise and did I say funny?"
—Henry Winkler, Actor, Author, Producer

"Barbara Paskoff is one of the wittiest, funniest and most entertaining women I know -- and this says a lot from someone who knows Sarah Silverman, Amy Schumer and Whitney Cummings! I am a huge fan of her way with words, and the table of contents of this book is the story of my life at age 54. Thanks, Barbara and Carol, for writing about women like me in a humorous and irreverent way!!!"
—Lisa Lampanelli, Comedian, Writer, Actor

"It was once said, "After 60, expect with everything you have two of—one won't work properly." In Paskoff and Pack's *Over-Sixty: Shades of Gray*, they make it quite clear that although body and mind stuff begin changing at 60, there's still hope. An injection of fun, decent health and a positive mindset can serve us well. They persuade us that approaching 70 can be the new fifty. Almost. The guide pulls no punches in the aging battle. It offers practical advice, humorous anecdotes and direct medical approaches. *Over-Sixty: Shades of Gray* makes turning 60-plus almost tolerable! Paskoff and Pack expose the "dirty little secrets" of aging—and help us laugh about them … while teaching us not to be afraid."
—Vin Di Bona, Creator, America's Funniest Videos

"Come young, come old and those who try to hide their age by plastic surgery! Pack and Paskoff have penned the ultimate hilarious roadmap on how to survive everyone's inevitable journey into the future."
—Linda Kenney Baden, Trial Attorney, Author

"If you ever got the feeling your stuff strutted off without you, *Over-Sixty: Shades of Gray* is for you. Finally, a truly useful guide to getting older, which is marinated in humor, rather than pity. Pack and Paskoff do us a great service, while keeping us laughing. The moral? Just because we're playing on the back nine, doesn't mean we can't finish up strong."
—Leslie Gold, The Radiochick, Broadcaster

"Hilarious and wonderful! To be scientifically sound AND humorous at the same time—and well-written—is a great accomplishment. They've come to terms with what is now a global phenomenon, and they are offering seriously good advice."
—Ambassador Edward Nell, AMB to the United Nations

"This book is practical, funny and filled with understandable, everyday conversation; the way we speak to each other as friends. After all, this is what life is about, right, getting to know one another over food, drinks and laughter. *Over-Sixty: Shades of Gray* is filled with witty, charismatic, authentic humor; the rare kind!"
—Tony Dovolani, Dancing With The Stars

Over-Sixty:
Shades of Gray

A Journey Through Life's Later Years
(ON THE ROAD TO FOSSILIZATION)

by

Barbara Paskoff & Carol Pack

Artiqua Press

www.artiquapress.com

EMMA S. CLARK MEMORIAL LIBRARY
Setauket, L.I., New York 11733

No part of this publication may be reproduced, distributed, or transmitted in any form or by any means, including photocopying, recording, or other electronic, digital, or mechanical methods, without the prior written permission of the publisher, except in the case of brief quotations embodied in critical reviews and certain other noncommercial uses permitted by copyright law. For permission requests, contact the publisher with "Attention: Permissions Coordinator" in the subject line.

ARTIQUA PRESS
www.artiquapress.com
info@artiquapress.com
Westbury, NY 11590

TRADE PAPERBACK

September 25, 2018

OVER-SIXTY: SHADES OF GRAY
A Journey Through Life's Later Years
(On the Road to Fossilization)

Copyright © 2018 Carol Pack, Barbara Paskoff
All rights reserved.

ISBN-13: 978-1-970028-02-7

Library of Congress Control Number: 2018938440

ABOUT OUR BOOK

There is no getting around it: With every breath we take, we are a couple of seconds older than we were before—and there is no turning back! It was fine when we were children and couldn't wait to grow up, but it's kind of horrifying now—for those of us over sixty—when the younger generations start to look at us differently. As far as a lot of young people are concerned, older men and women are disposable because they are hopelessly out of sync with today's world and cost the government too many tax dollars.

So many of the things older adults take for granted change dramatically with age. And these changes can be very disturbing. A lot of us unnecessarily suffer in silence, thinking what we are experiencing is somehow our fault. The doctors interviewed for this book claim many of their patients are too embarrassed to ask important personal questions. *Over-Sixty: Shades of Gray—A Journey Through Life's Later Years* is not embarrassed to both ask and answer these questions. The book provides sixty-plussers with a more positive perspective of themselves and offers expert guidance on how to navigate the aging process.

According to the last census, close to sixty million people in the United States are sixty or older. That's a lot of gray hair and bad teeth. A United Nations World Population report predicts that by the year 2045, people sixty or older will outnumber children under the age of fifteen. Humankind is getting older.

Writer/producer Normal Lear has rightly said, "Seniors are the lost demographic." We wrote *Over-Sixty: Shades of Gray* as a self-help book specifically for sixty-plussers. We want our readers to believe they are still relevant because they are still relevant. After all, the over-sixty demographic has the greatest life experience, immeasurable wisdom, and the most disposable income, too. We are simultaneously a force to be reckoned with and indispensable to the younger generation.

While we were researching this book, we often found ourselves smiling. Why? Because so many of our own questions were being answered. Many people over sixty assume their problems are unique, but there is always someone, somewhere, experiencing the same setbacks or adjusting to the same symptoms of aging.

We are passionate about *Over-Sixty: Shades of Gray* because it stems from our own experiences in navigating olderhood.

> O is for olfactory glands that fail us
> L is for the life we've lived to date
> D is for depression that may strike us
> E means elderly, a word we hate
> R is for retirement, so sleep late
> H is for the hair loss we may see
> O is for how ornery we're feeling
> O —another "o"—you're killing me…
> D is for the dread we face in aging
> 'Cause we're getting close to the last mile
> So, we wrote *Over-Sixty: Shades of Gray*
> To help us face the future with a smile.

An old adage says, "Write what you know." When it comes to *Over-Sixty: Shades of Gray*, we wrote about our experiences. It isn't Shakespeare, but there is definitely a method to our madness. Within the pages of this book, we hope our readers will unearth a wealth of insight and practical information about the changes occurring in their own lives.

> *"Always remember that you are unique, just like everyone else."*
> —Margaret Mead

TABLE OF CONTENTS:

Perception/Perspectives

This section addresses the mindset of men and women as they age— their feelings about time growing shorter, re-adjusting daily routines, and the stark realization of life's finality. But there are also lessons to be learned that make the transition to olderhood a whole lot smoother.

Sexuality

This section focuses on the challenges of an aging body and its effect on sexuality and relationships.

C & C

Being diagnosed with cancer or cardiovascular disease can be devastating. In this section we document many personal experiences on the medical front. We speak, too, with physicians who answer many of the questions posed by their patients.

Five Senses

This section examines the role our five senses—smell, sight, taste, hearing, and touch—play in our lives.

Mouthing Off

Our mouths are a constant source of pleasure and pain. Whether it's the joy of eating something wonderful, or experiencing problems chewing it, what passes our lips has a lot of control over our lives.

Digestive Dissonance

This section examines our natural waste disposal system, which sometimes doesn't work the way we expect it to—and that sucks!

Not Done Yet

The inevitable changes that accompany aging bodies and minds dramatically impact many men and women over sixty. This section addresses what those changes are and includes expert advice from a pharmacist and two psychologists on coping with and managing problems associated with them.

Image & Self Esteem

In this section we explore how the people we once were have morphed into individuals we no longer recognize.

Other Stuff

Once you pack your bag for a vacation and have all the essentials you need, you might want to throw in a couple of extra items to make your suitcase even more inclusive. That's what this section includes.

Mal-Contents

This section addresses the phenomenon of former valuable possessions becoming less valuable and more of a hindrance.

Tech-NO-logy

This section acknowledges the critical technological adjustments that come with aging.

Invested

Living on a fixed income can be scary. We develop spending patterns when we are working that are extremely hard to break when we are no longer receiving weekly paychecks. This section looks at some of the ways we can stretch our limited dollars and put our personal affairs in order to protect our loved ones.

Social Studies

In this section, we share ideas on how to take that first step to a more fulfilling life.

Dead End

Nobody likes going to funerals, least of all his or her own. This section shows how a little planning can go a long way in helping us rest in peace.

Memory Lane

This section takes a stroll down memory lane.

Other Voices

In this final section, we asked some of our friends how they feel about aging.

Acknowledgments

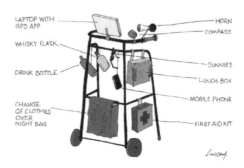

THE WALKING FRAME FOR THE MOBILE IMMOBILE

Perception
&
Perspectives

Essay No. 1

CONSIDER THE ~~GRAY~~ SILVER LINING:

Not broken capillaries—the second blush of youth.

Not cellulite—baby fat.

Not dentures—straight, even teeth.

Not belching—expressing respect for a good meal.

Not wrinkles—character.

Not old—wise.

Not fat—substantial.

Not fallen arches—making good contact with the ground.

Not balding—divested.

Not gray—fair haired.

Not liver spots—beauty marks.

Not forgetful—concentrating on other things.

Not arthritis—biofeedback.

Not shorter—more compact.

Essay No. 2

AM I LOSING MY MIND?

If you are anything like me—and thousands of other people—you have walked into a room and wondered why you were there. I become flustered, frustrated, and sometimes panicky, and wonder if I'm in the early stages of dementia.

Fortunately, we may have little reason to panic. Clinical psychologist Jerry Gold says: "If you walk into the kitchen and see the fridge and you know it's the fridge, you're good. It's when you walk into the kitchen and see the fridge and ask, 'What is this?' that you have a problem." More than likely, you are allowing yourself to become distracted. We all lead busy lives with various people, events, and situations diverting our attention—not to mention e-mails, phone calls, and television. Distractions can feed a vicious cycle—starting one thing, becoming distracted and going on to another thing, and then becoming distracted again and going on to yet another thing. It happens to me most often when I'm cleaning. Ask any professional housecleaner and he or she will tell you that dusting shelves and mopping floors is mindless work that invites daydreaming. So, it's no surprise that we are thinking of something else when we return a pair of shoes to the bedroom closet and become distracted by something out of place in the bedroom. And so it goes from room to room. I think of it as the *pinball syndrome*. We are all over the place during the execution of our task, but we eventually do reach the end.

I have friends who have done odd things when they have lost concentration—like trying to use the TV remote as a cell phone or throwing a face towel in the toilet and toilet paper in the tub. According to Dr. Gold: With all the outside stimuli we have to contend with and all the multitasking we do, we are bound to lose concentration.

Still, we have a tendency to become frustrated with ourselves for being so forgetful. I know I get scared when I forget about turning off the teakettle or the running water in the tub. That kind of forgetfulness can cause major damage.

But all of us have probably forgotten someone's name or where we parked the car at one time or another. Age has nothing to do with it. Besides, do you feel old? I bet you don't. I remember my grandmother saying her body may have aged but, in her mind, she would always be an eighteen-year-old girl. That's a good age to be. And there are some things we can do to preserve our memories so we don't forget what our younger selves were like. According to clinical psychologist Ann Lane, crossword puzzles and other brain stimuli help keep us sharp. Regular socializing, too, helps ward off depression and stress that could distract us. And getting at least eight hours of sleep helps our minds sort through our memories, so we can remember them when we need to remember them.

We could also keep a calendar to help us remember important dates. I have one that wirelessly connects to my computer, iPad, and cell phone. It alerts me to appointments and meetings an hour in advance. There is this salesman I once knew who used to sit in his car after every meeting with a client and write down anything new he learned about that person or his or her business on an index card. When he later asked about a grandson's graduation or a sister's new home, his clients marveled at his recall. All he had to do to enhance his memory was reread the index cards prior to meeting with his clients. There's nothing wrong with keeping notes. It works.

And then there's music. Just playing our favorite songs from our youth can be invigorating. Who doesn't dance around the kitchen when they hear their favorite tune? Music can soothe, excite, and reawaken forgotten memories. It can kick start the brain when we are feeling fuzzy. So, add music to your mental gymnastics and start exercising your brain to keep from losing your mind.

Most of us have the ability of "total recall." We just need to preplan and use cues and mind games. Will we remember the water is running in the tub? Maybe, if we sing a song like Bobby Darren's "Splish Splash" until we shut it off. Or make it a point to never leave the bathroom if the water is running. Preplanning. We have to remember to not be forgetful.

Of all the things I've lost I miss my mind the most. —Ozzy Osbourne

Essay No. 3

"He's still in denial."

WHAT'S THE HURRY?

If you are sixty years old and—in your mind—have an end point of one hundred years, you have forty more years to go. Assuming, of course, you live to be one hundred. You may have experienced a number of health bumps along the way, but as far as you know, you are fine right now. While writing this chapter, I turned seventy-three. Living to be one hundred seems unrealistic to me and death seems more immediate. I am aware that this kind of thinking is viewed by some as an emotionally unproductive way to go through one's *golden years*. It's not an *oh-my-god-I'm-going-to-die-soon* feeling, but more like a cloud hanging over me. As one unknown author said, "Today is the last day of some of your life."

When I was growing up in New York City, I would often go to Schrafft's, a chain of moderately priced restaurants that dotted the city streets on both the east and west sides of Central Park. It is where the ladies lunched. The restaurants were huge with very long soda fountain service areas where *single* women could grab something to eat. All the kids would go to Schrafft's after school and have ice cream sundaes. Their hot fudge was so wonderfully thick and rich that it would harden on the metal spoon after dipping it into the freezing cold ice cream. What kid cared about calories? We were young. There was always tomorrow. Stuff like that was for older folks to worry about.

For many young people, getting older is a goal that takes too long to reach. They feel stuck in the moment. It's a fact: Being young comes with limitations on what one can and cannot do. And that makes time drag. Children want to get older in order to do more things. From a child's perspective, being young is a disadvantage. That's how it felt for me. For example, I couldn't wait for summer. The anticipation was exhausting. When summer finally arrived, it was over in a blink of an eye. I couldn't wait to be a teenager and then an adult. The thought of being older was exhilarating. And the older I got the more excited I became. I was getting closer to what I saw as freedom.

And so, the years kept passing and then one day—just like that—I looked back and saw my childhood, teenage years, and early adulthood become nothing more than memory markers of time gone by. The older I became, the more surprised I was at the speed in which time traveled. I am how old? Already?

Today, even with many days of the week seeming to be at a standstill, time still marches on. The clock and the calendar continue their journeys forward. There are times when I can honestly admit to feeling panicked. If I start something, I need to finish it *now* because time is a real concern. Anticipatory anxiety is both exhausting and scary. That's my hurry. My *freedom* has been replaced with a sense of urgency. And forever doesn't seem to be forever enough.

When you don't want time to pass, it feels like it's moving faster. And we feel rushed to accomplish what we need to accomplish. So, I guess the one thing about time is this: We experience *the want* in the opposite way. But if we look too far back or look too far in the future, we will certainly miss the now. And who knows how much longer the now is?

Guest Essay No. 4

WILL THIS BE MY LAST?
by Carol Scibelli

Two years ago, I bought the washer and dryer pictured above. Of course, they weren't sold with the laundry in them. I announced to friends: "This is probably the last washer and dryer I will ever buy!" I didn't say it to be morbid. I read the warranty and I did the math. Those younger than me scoffed at that, but anyone my age or older paused—probably to watch the highlights of their lives pass before them—and then they made a few cheery statements of their own.

"If I buy my next car and keep it until it conks—that may be my final car or maybe one more. If I lease for thirty-six months, that works out to four more cars. That feels better—although, before I know it my kids or the cops will probably take away my license and tell me it's for my own good."

"I no longer check off 'three years' for subscriptions. It's not a bargain if you're dead."

"Last house. It's condo living for us. And, of course, no steps. This means I will never again say, "Let's go upstairs." Oh no...

When I *celebrated* turning s-s-sixty, I realized something startling. I may be too old for certain things but there is nothing I'm too young for. Oh my...

Have a nice day, fellow baby boomers.

Originally published in October 2012 by *Poor Widow Me*

"I'M LOOKING SERIOUSLY
INTO CRYOGENICS

LIFE'S A BITCH

We all must deal with loss, which can be pretty devastating at times, even though we are often introduced to it fairly early in life. There is a reason why life insurance isn't sold for goldfish. Not that the typical seven-year-old realizes how temporary his little finned friend's life is to begin with, but life has a deadline. Even radioactive isotopes with long half-lives eventually bite the dust. Knowing this doesn't make accepting loss any easier. Indeed, as we get older and our peers start dying off, our sense of loss is profound.

In my teens, I lost a grandfather whom I cherished. For the first four years of my life, my family and I lived with my grandparents. Papa was always waiting in the kitchen when I woke up at the crack of dawn. He would make me breakfast and, afterwards, sit me on his knee and read me the comic strips in broken English. He was my hero.

In my twenties, my pregnant best friend died of toxemia. In my thirties, I lost my four-year-old son in a car accident. That was the most devastating loss of all. Your children are supposed to bury you, not the other way around. I cut myself off from every friend I ever had because I didn't want to talk with them about his death. So, I not only lost a son, but also every friend in my unorganized support group.

When it came time for my son's wake, my husband—who suffers profound anxiety over being in a room with a dead person—spent three days sitting alone in the waiting room of the funeral home.

His best friend died of a drug overdose a short time later. When that happened, he drove me to the wake and sent me inside in his place. It wasn't easy paying condolences, or explaining why my husband wasn't there, to a widow who did not speak English. She was from Bolivia and didn't have much family here. While my husband sat out in the car, the most I could do was give her a hug and say a prayer before the coffin.

As I got older, the rate of loss increased. I come from a large, extended Italian family, so there were plenty of older relatives with whom I spent every major holiday. I had a deep well of separation anxiety to draw from. However, each time someone close to me died, it prepared me a little more for dealing with the next loss.

Now for the embarrassing truth: One of the ways I deal with death is giggling. I need to break the tension. I didn't giggle at my son's funeral, but I may have felt better if I had. Giggling looks disrespectful. But is it?

Probably the easiest way to deal with loss is to believe in reincarnation. If it works for Shirley MacLaine, why shouldn't it work for all of us? And it could help some of us face our own limited life spans. Whether we come back one time, or seven, believing in life after death, for me, is a sure way of reducing the fear factor. It's either that or, taking a page from Ted Williams's book, arranging to be cryogenically frozen before our expiration dates.

*"Do not take life too seriously,
you will never get out of it alive."*
— Elbert Hubbard

I'm writing my memoirs. Can you remember
what we've been doing for the past forty years?

EVERYONE HAS A PAST

I sometimes wonder when younger people look at us if they ever see beyond the obvious. Do they have any idea that we were once young, and that we were where they are today? They don't realize that one day they will be where we are now.

They don't know that I was a tomboy—that I played softball and touch football. That I used to cut school and go to my boyfriend's house to make out. And that I cried for weeks when we broke up. That I was in the first ever Miss Teenage America Contest and was one of the ten finalists in New York State. That I used to sneak a cigarette with my friend in her bathroom and blow the smoke out the window, then spray the room with perfume so we wouldn't leave any telltale signs. That I used to hang out on the street corner and wear a silver clip in my hair because that was cool.

They also don't know that I cheated on tests in high school to get better grades. My parents wouldn't have been happy if I didn't. That I had to go to summer school to get into college because I was the class clown in high school and, like I said, cheated on tests to get better grades. They also don't know that I did get into college and was voted junior prom queen. And I graduated without cheating on one test. Then, of course, like most of my contemporaries, I married, had a child, and began life's next chapter.

One day their life experiences will season them. And they will look at their reflections in the mirror and say, "We are much more than what you see!"

"The past is never where you think you left it."
—Katherine Anne Porter

Sexuality

"NEED... SKIN MOISTURIZER..."

DRY EYE, DRY SKIN, DRY VAGINA

Having a vagina is a tremendous responsibility. It should look pretty. It should smell pretty. It should function. But as we age, pretty—not so much; odorous—maybe more so; and function—well that's another story.

Have you ever taken a mirror and stuck it between your legs to see what's going on down there? Well, I have. It's an interesting piece of anatomy. It looks like a mussel without the shell—a self-portrait if you will. When I was younger it was tighter, pinker, and had muscle tone. My vagina was a playful little darling. It would swell at the thought of romance with anyone.

Today my vagina yearns for lubrication of the Vaseline kind. I have tried olive oil, Wesson oil, vitamin E oil. Even my husband has gotten into lubing and oiling up to help make intercourse easier. But dry is still dry. So, I have named my vagina "Sahara."

Let me digress for a moment to tell you a joke. Unfortunately, I have no recollection of who said it, but it wasn't me. Here goes: "An older man goes to the doctor nervous as can be. The doctor asks him what the problem is. The older man says, 'Doctor, my penis is purple.' 'Hmmm,' the doctor responds. 'Are you sexually active?' The man replies, 'Yes.' The doctor asks, 'Do you have intercourse often?' The older man responds, 'Enough.' The doctor asks, 'Do you use a lubricant?' The man responds: 'Yes. Jelly.' The doctor asks, 'What kind?' The older man looks at the doctor, pauses for a second, then says, 'Grape!'"

Enough about that, now back to me. Just like the rest of me, *down there* has an image problem. "Sahara" is not so tight and that little tongue that sticks out between the lips and stands at attention has now, like my neck, loosened and dropped. I feel bad, sometimes less womanly, but I soldier on. You should know, I am not screaming during sex from joy!

As with everything else, my hormones—according to my gynecologist—are partially to blame. Even though I may not need an abundance of them—since my days of making babies have long since sailed—I wouldn't mind the feeling of moist once in a while. And that goes for my eyes and skin as well. And while I'm on the subject of dry, let me add my mouth, my feet, my cuticles, and my hair. You get the picture.

*"Older women are like aging strudels—
the crust may be not so lovely, but
the filling has come at last into its own."*
—Robert Farrar Capon

GYNECOLOGIST WENDY FRIED SAYS:

LUBRICATION:

- THERE ARE TWO CATEGORIES OF LUBRICANTS: WATER SOLUBLE AND OIL BASED.
- IF YOU USE A CONDOM, USE A WATER-SOLUBLE LUBRICANT LIKE ASTROGLIDE OR K-Y JELLY.
- OIL BASED IS FINE IF YOU ARE NOT USING A CONDOM.

ODOR:

- IF YOU DETECT A FISHY ODOR, IT COULD BE A BACTERIAL INFECTION THAT SHOULD BE TREATED WITH ANTIBIOTICS.
- IF YOU SMELL AMMONIA, IT COULD BE FROM URINE LOSS.

Love song of the Baby boomer

SENIOR SEX

by Ann Lane, Psy.D.

It is commonly believed that sexual interest withers as we age. That's not necessarily so. Poor health, side effects of medications, and lack of a partner aside, diminished action in the bedroom can be attributed to some psychological barriers.

Initially, seniors are often reluctant to bring up the topic of sex. However, with a little nudging they are more than willing to discuss such feelings as embarrassment about sexual desires and fantasies, self-consciousness about their changing bodies, worries about performance, guilt, frustration with disinterested partners, and difficulty expressing their needs in bed.

Sometimes it's a challenge to help people break through these psychological blocks because negative attitudes have been deeply ingrained and are constantly reinforced by a society that places derogatory labels on senior sex. "Dirty old men," "horny old geezer," and "hot granny" are commonly used terms by our youth-oriented world. Roadblocks to sexual intimacy can be overcome by changing negative attitudes, developing realistic expectations, and self-acceptance.

The following are some tips to help continue, resume, or begin enjoying one's older but sexual self:

Dr. Ann Lane says:

- Yes, your body has changed, but so have your partners! Sexual pleasure has nothing to do with perky breasts and tight butts.
- Who cares what your adult kids think about mom and dad enjoying a romp in the bedroom!
- Speak up in bed. Learn what feels good and communicate it to your partner.
- If you don't have a partner, take care of yourself. It's good for stress reduction and a way of learning about your own body.
- Don't be afraid to try new things. Put those fantasies to good use. If your partner is shocked, he or she needs to work on his or her issues.

Dr. Wendy Fried says:

- When entering a new relation, both parties should be tested for Sexually Transmitted Diseases (STDs) like gonorrhea, chlamydia, HIV, HPV, syphilis, and herpes.
- Use a condom because—even though you can't get pregnant—you are still at risk for STDs.
- Don't be reluctant to talk with your gynecologist about sex. They've heard it all.
- If you want to get your horny on and it's just not coming, blame it on your hormones and watch porn.

GOOD VIBRATIONS

What I didn't dare think about or do in the fifties, sixties, and seventies, I made up for in the eighties, nineties, and new millennium. Who during the fifties, sixties, and seventies considered playing with himself or herself? As a matter of fact, it was rarely discussed. I'm a product of that old school where the joke was, "If you play with yourself you'll go blind." The response: "Then how 'bout until I need glasses!" For the record, I'm wearing glasses.

Now a senior and a veteran of long-term therapy, I have a sense of security—a freedom with my fantasies and horniness, no matter how outrageous they both are. At first, I was embarrassed by my fantasies. But in time I learned to accept them. After all, they are part of who I am. And the bottom line is this: Fantasies are just fantasies and keeping them as just fantasies is safe.

Years ago, I had a sexual appetite that, like my husband, gave me a perpetual hard-on. They were my horny years. They were my vibrator years. I had a lover with a fifteen-inch cord. It all seemed very exciting. The newness. The intensity. The one-to-three speed options.

Today my fantasies are fewer but my horniness—or lack thereof—still gives me a jolt at times. I still have that vibrator. We still use that vibrator. As a matter of fact, we have become a steady trio.

Orgasms are nice. They really are. I used to love them. I used to love thinking about them. They felt good. They released tension. But I don't have orgasms that often anymore. I should. Having them is good for the brain. I have been told that orgasms release serotonin, the happy chemicals in the brain. I am aware that it's more complicated than that, but the bottom line is: Having an orgasm is a high.

Years ago, when I put the vibrator *there*, *there* would know what to do. These days, the biggest problem with having an orgasm is all the work I have to *do* to make it happen. Now it's about: I'll move it here. Put it there. No here. Yes, that's it! YES! Yes! … Lost it!

Sex is a schlep! I'd rather watch television.

Nothing else that I am aware of should interfere with me having an orgasm. My estrogen levels have been tested. They are below sea level. I don't take any meds that would have an effect on my sex life. I don't have any diseases and I'm not depressed. Of course, I experience stress every so often, but who doesn't?

Hormone replacement therapy is available for relief; it's been around for ages. But do I want to take a chance with the side effects? So, the question remains: Hormones or not to moan!

I can just imagine the evening news teasing the oncoming hour: They have been in bed over an hour. It's 11 p.m. She is still trying to have that orgasm. Stay tuned. We'll tell you how she did. All that and more coming soon!

Dr. Wendy Fried says:

- Masturbation is physically and emotionally healthy for women of all ages... and men, too.
- Vibrators of any kind, both external and internal, are for the most part safe and effective.
- Thorough cleaning between uses decreases the risk of infection.

I always listen to my doctor. I'm a very good patient (wink, wink) if you get my drift.

> "There are a number of mechanical devices which increase sexual arousal, particularly in women. Chief among these is the Mercedes-Benz 380SL convertible."
> —P. J. O'Rourke

C & C

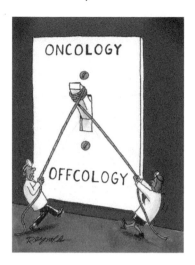

WHAT IS THIS THING CALLED CANCER?

When you get diagnosed with cancer things change. A LOT. Everything becomes different. Feelings become different. The way you see and hear things become different. You think about your mortality and whether you are going to live or die. You think about the emotional and physical pain and the de-humanizing evolution of the disease. The physical and emotional morphing into this *other* person literally brings you to your knees.

Is that the legacy I wanted to leave my daughter? I was so scared for her. And what about my husband? What would it be like for him if I died? I was so worried about my daughter and husband's feelings of hopelessness and powerlessness.

How is it that we are here one moment and gone the next? What kind of sadistic tease is that?

I went underground after my cancer diagnosis. I hardly spoke to or saw anyone. It was a welcome relief. I didn't have to see the pain in the faces of family and friends. Or listen to them groping for the right words.

I was protecting myself from feeling more horrible than I already did. Also, I wondered—if by association—they were experiencing anticipatory anxiety at the thought of one day having to deal with a diagnosis of their own. Minute by minute and day by day, I was exhausted trying to wrap my head around this. My aloneness became my cocoon—my safe haven. It was emotional survival.

There is something about this damn cancer and how it takes on a life of its own. If you let it, cancer can own you.

If individuals in your life are diagnosed with cancer and decide to push those around them away, try not to take it personally. It's not that they don't care about you. They are trying to muster up the strength to be strong for you. Even with all I was going through, there was always that pull to take care of others—and make them believe I was strong and capable of handling whatever blow I was dealt—so *they* wouldn't feel bad. That's a heavy and exhausting burden.

The feeling of loss of control—the powerlessness and vulnerability—is all consuming. It's palpable not only for me, but also for my friends who felt pushed aside. Everyone wanted to help and say the right thing. But unless they had a magic wand it was wasted energy.

To the best of my knowledge there was no one in my immediate family who had breast cancer. Other cancers, perhaps, but not breast cancer.

Without missing a beat, I went for my mammogram and sonogram every year. Because I was terrified to go alone, my husband would accompany me.

I was sixty-three when I was first diagnosed. I had only two risk factors—being older and being a woman. I am well aware that women of all ages are diagnosed with breast cancer. But men, too, can develop it. About 2,000 men are diagnosed annually and approximately 450 of them will die of the disease. According to the American Cancer Society (ACS), your risk for breast cancer increases as you age. The ACS says about 77 percent of women diagnosed with breast cancer are over fifty, and almost half are sixty-five and older. Approximately 75 percent of all breast cancers are diagnosed in women *without* any risk factors.

I remember years ago, when I was a broadcast journalist, being stunned when interviewing a twenty-six-year-old woman. She had had a double mastectomy. So, who knows?

I had an incredible support system. It helped me get through the diagnosis, the double mastectomy, which was my choice, and chemo, with all its awful side effects. My brain was on pause. I couldn't think logically. I couldn't construct an intelligent sentence. My oncologist called it *chemo brain.* I called it a "terrorized brain." What's interesting is that I never remember saying, "Why me?" Well, maybe just once. But that was it. It was always more about saying, "HOW?"

My prognosis was good, although I was very unsure of the future and what it would hold. But as the time passed from the day of my diagnosis to now—ten years later—I can say without hesitation: *I am good.* The more time that goes by, the more confident I become that there will be many more tomorrows.

I never looked at being diagnosed with breast cancer as a "gift." I know a lot of women do. Perhaps it's their way of coping with the horror of it all and having to make sense of it. I don't know. I personally never got that aspect of it.

One thing I have tried to do is not let it define me. The last thing I wanted was pity. I tried not to let it take over who I was and who I hoped to continue to be. What I did discover was the intense caring of the breast cancer community. Doctors, nurses, health care professionals, support groups, and patients themselves are there for you every step of the way. I have been very fortunate.

SURGEON KAREN KOSTROFF SAYS:

- FOR MOST PEOPLE, BREAST CANCER IS A HIGHLY CURABLE DISEASE.
- THE SOONER A PATIENT COLLECTS TREATMENT INFORMATION, THE SOONER THEY WILL FEEL IN CONTROL AND LESS TERRIFIED.
- ALWAYS BRING A FAMILY MEMBER OR FRIEND TO THE DOCTOR SO THE PATIENT CAN CONCENTRATE ON LISTENING, AND THE FAMILY MEMBER/FRIEND CAN TAKE NOTES AND ASK ADDITIONAL QUESTIONS.
- PATIENTS SHOULD ASK THE FOLLOWING QUESTIONS: WHAT TREATMENTS ARE AVAILABLE? HOW MUCH TREATMENT IS REQUIRED? HOW LONG IS THE RECOVERY TIME?
- ASK YOUR DOCTOR WHAT HE OR SHE WOULD DO IN THE SAME SITUATION.

OVERCOMING THE FEAR FACTOR
by Ann Lane, Psy.D.

1.　　Identify your fears: The greater your awareness, the better chance you have of overcoming fear. Unacknowledged fears tend to express themselves in self-sabotage, procrastination, lack of follow-through, rationalizations, avoidance, anxieties, and a constant state of self-dissatisfaction.

2.　　Assess each fear:　Fear is an EMOTIONAL response. THINKING is a cognitive process that allows us to look at things unemotionally. When we are not in the grip of powerful emotions, we are better able to understand what is going on and approach situations more realistically.

3.　　Set some goals:　Choose one goal at a time and develop a detailed plan to achieve it. Create smaller sub-goals that are less anxiety provoking. With each accomplished step your confidence will rise and fears diminish.

4.　　Challenge your negative thoughts: "I can't do it," "They will laugh at me," and "I'm not that smart" are thoughts that will squash your motivation. Replace them with "Trying is not going to kill me," "If I don't succeed I can improve my skill," and "This may be tough but it's worth the effort."

5.　　How many relationships, jobs, projects, and other opportunities have you allowed to slip by because of fears? Fears can rob you of many life-enhancing experiences. Take control and work towards removing fears from your path so you can live a fuller, richer, and happier life.

Reprinted with permission from *Harford's Heart* magazine

"You got a better idea? The paddles are
BROKEN. Just turn the key."

YA GOTTA HAVE HEART

A number of years ago I co-produced a documentary on women and
heart disease called *A Woman's Heart,* which aired on PBS. What an eye
opener that was. Who knew that heart attacks were—and still are—
the leading cause of death in women in the United States. Approximately 300,000 women die annually from heart attacks. Many of
the physicians we spoke with said one major reason women didn't
excessively worry about heart disease was their fear of getting breast
cancer. For them getting breast cancer posed the greater risk. Heart
disease wasn't typically on their radar. It certainly wasn't on my mind.

The majority of women believed heart attacks occurred mostly in men.
If a woman experienced any heart-related symptoms, she would more
often than not dismiss them with a benign diagnosis like heartburn, gas,
muscle spasms, and even anxiety, which many health care professionals
would diagnose their female patients as having. The cardiologists we
spoke with told us that most clinical studies were done on men. So, the
many things we learned about heart disease—and the drugs used to
stem its dangers—came from studies involving mostly men. However,
biased as this may sound, they said the reasoning was legitimate and

cautionary. The fear of exposing unborn children to experimental drugs led to the exclusion of women in their childbearing years. Older women who were more likely to be at risk were also excluded.

What angered me so much during the filming of the documentary was the prejudice in the medical community about women and heart disease. If a woman complained about symptoms to her physician, she would often be sent home with the diagnosis that it was all in her head.

We interviewed a forty-year-old woman whom I'll call "Susan." For weeks, Susan was suffering from what she thought was indigestion. She kept taking antacids but to no avail. One night the pain became so unbearable that Susan called 911. When the paramedics arrived, they thought she was doing drugs. They had no idea that a forty-year-old woman complaining of heart attack symptoms might actually be having a heart attack. And they still didn't believe her when she flat-out denied ever having taken drugs. But the accusations continued. After examining her—and still under the impression she was using—they made her walk alone up into the ambulance. When Susan finally arrived at the hospital she passed out and had to be resuscitated on two occasions. She survived the heart attack, but not without cost. Because of the delay earlier that day, Susan developed congestive heart failure. According to cardiologist Stacey Rosen, when women have heart disease they are often left with a weakened heart muscle. They are alive, but they are unable to do all their previous activities. To watch someone die of long-standing heart disease is as crippling and horrible as watching someone expire from cancer.

I don't know what became of Susan. We kept in touch for a while, but eventually lost contact. I will always remember her for her bravery and ability to forgive.

Thankfully so much has changed since then. Experts say research has broadened medical professionals' awareness and understanding of gender differences in the origin of the disease, diagnosis, treatment, and prevention.

Yet heart disease still remains the leading cause of death for both men and women. According to the American Heart Association, 720,000 Americans will have a heart attack and about 600,000 will die of the disease.

The cardiologists we spoke with said no one age group is immune to heart disease. The fact is, a family history and getting older does increase one's risk of developing heart problems. Just like so many other parts of our body that slow down and change as we age, our hearts are no exception. And for women, the loss of hormones after menopause also increases the risk.

The doctors also explained that it's important to understand that heart disease is not just one disease. It encompasses many different heart health issues. Coronary artery disease, often referred to as CAD, can include heart failure, chest pains, and irregular heartbeat, known as arrhythmia. If these critical health issues aren't addressed, and blood flow is reduced or blocked altogether from a section of heart muscle, that part of the muscle dies. And that is a heart attack.

"As sobering as these facts are," cardiologist Jennifer Mieres says, "there are reasons to be optimistic. No matter how old you are, knowing the risk factors that are in your control is the key to prevention. And making the necessary changes is one of the most effective weapons we have in fighting heart disease."

According to Cardiologist Stacey Rosen:

- If you smoke, STOP. Experts agree that smoking is the number one preventable cause of death.
- Monitor your cholesterol and high blood pressure numbers. If you take medication don't stop.
- Check your sugar level to monitor diabetes.
- Maintain a healthy body weight.
- Get enough exercise—at least thirty minutes of exercise daily.

- Reduce alcohol consumption.
- Find healthy outlets to relieve stress.
- Eat a heart-healthy diet—fruits, veggies, high-fiber from whole grains. Choose foods that are low in salt and fat.
- Get enough sleep.
- If you do have a family history of heart disease, make aggressive lifestyle changes.

The symptoms of a heart attack vary from person to person. Not everyone experiences a heart attack in the same way. Men and women often experience symptoms very differently from one another.

TYPICAL SYMPTOMS BY GENDER	
MALE	FEMALE
CHEST PAINS	CHEST PAINS
RADIATING PAIN	RADIATING PAIN
PRESSURE	PRESSURE
LIGHT HEADED	LIGHT HEADED
NAUSEA	NAUSEA
PERSPIRATION	PERSPIRATION
	SEVERE BREATHLESSNESS
	STOMACH PAIN
	BACK PAIN
	BELCHING
	PALPITATION
	INABILITY TO THINK CLEARLY

According to the American Heart Association, half the men who die suddenly of coronary heart disease had no previous symptoms.

WHAT YOU NEED TO ASK YOUR CARDIOLOGIST:

- RISK FACTORS
- BLOOD PRESSURE
- CHOLESTEROL
- BODY MASS
- BLOOD SUGAR LEVEL

80% OF HEART DISEASE IS PREVENTABLE:

- DON'T SMOKE.
- EAT PLENTY OF FRUITS, VEGETABLES, AND FIBER.
- CUT OUT SALT, FAT, AND SUGARY FOODS.
- WALKING EVERY DAY CAN MAKE A HUGE IMPACT.
- IT'S NEVER TOO EARLY TO START.

FIVE SENSES

Not including: Horse Sense, Common Sense,
Sixth Sense, Lick of Sense,
or Sense of Humor

"My nose smells."

OH, OH, OH, THOSE OLFACTORY GLANDS

Have you ever smelled something that took you back to another time in your life? When that exact same aroma was part of a wonderful memory? Okay, if you stepped in something and the odor is coming from the bottom of your shoe, maybe it's not so great. But you get the idea. The point is our olfactory glands have a lot of power over us. They can control our minds, our muscles when we grimace at an unpleasant odor, and our taste buds—gotta love those taste buds—because our noses can discriminate among thousands of different aromas. Plus, our sense of smell can protect us. We know there's a problem when we smell smoke, or gas, or spoiled food. And, of course, odors can give us pleasure. Who doesn't like the scent of Thanksgiving turkey, fresh-baked chocolate chip cookies, or newly cut grass? One of my favorites—baby powder—always makes me smile.

Unfortunately, the American Academy of Otolaryngology says that once we pass sixty our olfactory glands "retire," and we no longer discriminate between odors. When our sense of smell declines, so does our taste. Our taste buds may still differentiate between sweet, salty, bitter, and sour. But without the ability to discern aromas, food loses its flavor. Perhaps we won't realize it, but there will be signs. We might add more salt, or sugar, to a recipe. Maybe we'll lose the enjoyment we have always felt when dining out. Now that we no longer relish the taste, we might lose weight because we'll eat less food. Or we may gain weight eating all the wrong foods because they are the ones we are still able to taste. Consider this: We usually can't taste our food when we have a cold because we can't smell with a stuffed nose.

While we're on the subject, let's talk about taste buds. Just like our sense of smell alerts us to the dangers of fire or gas, our taste buds can prevent us from eating something really foul. According to experts, the number of taste buds a person has varies from individual to individual. You could have anywhere between 2,000 and 10,000 taste buds, which would explain why some people seem to have no taste at all, at least when it comes to food. Apparently, the more taste buds you have the stronger food tastes. This explains why some people like asparagus more than I do. They obviously don't taste what I taste. That's all going to change because, just like people, taste buds retire after a certain age. According to the National Institute of Health, as we advance in age, the number of taste buds we have decreases. Maybe in a few years, I'll find the taste of goat cheese tolerable, rather than thinking it tastes like the smell of stinky feet. And don't underestimate the power of saliva, it helps, too. Yes, we can also blame our hormones, or lack thereof, for this change.

The decline of olfactory stimuli may have an important impact. Olfactory glands help men detect pheromones, and some people believe human pheromones arouse a man's sexual response. So, the loss of olfactory sensation above the belt may play a role below the belt. Who *nose*?

FACTOIDS:

- YOU CAN HAVE ANYWHERE FROM 2,000 TO 10,000 TASTE BUDS. IT DIFFERS FROM PERSON TO PERSON.
- THE MORE TASTE BUDS YOU HAVE, THE STRONGER FOOD TASTES.
- ONCE WE PASS SIXTY OUR TASTE BUDS ARE LESS DISCRIMINATING.
- EXPERIMENTING WITH HERBS AND SPICES CAN ENHANCE FLAVOR.
- MEDICATIONS CAN CHANGE THE WAY FOOD TASTES.

"Until you walk a mile in another man's moccasins you can't imagine the smell."

—Robert Byrne

NOW YOU SEE IT, NOW YOU DON'T

Can you believe how small the fine print is on everything these days? Just because they can print in eight-point fonts doesn't mean they should. Wait! You're telling me that's twelve-point font? Impossible.

When it comes to age-related vision problems, there's both good news and bad news. I always like to begin on a positive note. We reach a point when nearsightedness may reverse itself. I've been myopic since I was nine years old. As I got older, my vision got worse until I turned a certain age. Then it began reversing itself. I find I no longer need glasses to watch a movie on TV and that's great. My brother is the same way. He told me his vision started improving a few years back and he no longer requires glasses when he drives.

Now for the bad news. Reading fine print will only get worse. Doctors say that as we get older, we suffer a progressive decline in visual acuity. It happens to us whether we are nearsighted, farsighted, or have 20-20 vision. The neural transmitters in our eyes no longer work the way they used to because of increasing rigidity in the lens. And there's not much we can do about it—other than wear reading glasses.

You can always tell when someone is having a problem reading because you'll see them move the newspaper or book at arm's length, trying to find the right distance where everything will *hopefully* come into focus.

OPHTHALMOLOGIST LESLIE GOLDBERG SAYS:

- AS WE AGE, WE ARE AT GREATER RISK OF DEVELOPING FLOATERS, CATARACTS, AND MACULAR DEGENERATION, WHICH IS DETERIORATION OF THE RETINA.
- GREEN LEAFY VEGETABLE, CITRUS FRUITS, NUTS, AND WHOLE GRAINS CAN HELP PREVENT MACULAR DEGENERATION AND SLOW THE PROGRESSION OF CATARACTS AND KEEP YOUR EYES HEALTHY.
- WEAR PROTECTIVE LENSES FOR WORK AND PLAY, AND SUNGLASSES WHEN YOU ARE OUTSIDE.
- THROW AWAY OLD EYE MAKEUP AFTER THREE MONTHS.
- STOP SMOKING.
- EVEN IF YOU ARE NOT EXPERIENCING A PROBLEM, SEE AN EYE DOCTOR EVERY ONE TO TWO YEARS.

As Humphrey Bogart said in *Casablanca*, "Here's looking at you, kid."

"Yes, that was very loud, but I said
I wanted to hear your HEART!"

WHAT?

I remember when everyone warned us that playing loud rock music would affect our hearing. We scoffed at them. We called them old geezers. Who knew?

At first, I blamed cell phones. They were the devil. Sure, they're handy, and you can play Solitaire on them if you own a pair of bifocals, but the sound isn't pristine. Hands-free car phones are the worst with all the extraneous sound from inside the vehicle. And why does everyone have to mumble? And it's not just phones. Those skinny speakers in flat screen TVs make the audio sound awful. And one network in particular must think it's very edgy having characters speak faster than the speed of light. Thank God for closed captioning. My husband would listen to the TV with the volume set at twenty-five all the time. I needed to increase it to fifty. He kept telling me it was too loud, but I told him it was him.

It occurred to me I might have excess wax in my ears, so I used some drops to flush it out. But the drops had expired seven years before and my ears felt itchy. So, I went to an ear, nose, and throat (ENT) specialist. "No wax. No infection. You're losing your hearing." Talk about a rude awakening. Wait...don't talk about it because I probably won't understand half the words you're saying. In my mind, losing my hearing equates to losing my youth.

Audiologist Melanie Herzfeld says we have to stop thinking that way. She says: "Seniors still think of hearing aids as a sign of being old and that is in need changing. We need to consider hearing devices as helpers to maintain our ability to communicate, to aid in cognitive functioning and not so much a sign of falling apart. They maintain [our] ability to converse, to understand, to learn, rather than they are needed because of disability!"

I struggled with my hearing for months before seeking help. I would strain to listen to every word and try to decipher them in my brain. If I drew a blank, I would smile and nod as if I agreed with whatever the person I was speaking with had said. Lord knows what horrible things I may have agreed to. I finally picked myself up and found an audiologist to fit me for hearing aids. My first pair was tiny. You could barely tell I had them on. The battery compartment slid behind my ear—under my hair—and a thin transparent wire attached to the earpiece that disappeared inside my ear canal. They were hardly noticeable. Too bad they didn't help as much as I would have liked. So, I upped the ante. My second pair is larger, a bit more noticeable behind the ear, but they are big enough to have a telecoil inside of them, which means less feedback. And the optional Bluetooth remote I purchased with them streams TV and cell calls directly to my hearing aids. I can use that remote to blast the volume as loud as I want without affecting the overall volume of the TV for everyone else. It's great for my home life. But isn't blasting the volume what got me in this predicament in the first place? Not necessarily. Herzfeld says hearing impairment has many possible causes.

HERZFELD SAYS:

- MEDICATIONS, DRUGS, GENETICS, ACCIDENTS, NOISE, DISEASE, AND AGING CAN ALL CAUSE HEARING IMPAIRMENT.
- HEARING AIDS HELP WITH COMMUNICATING. IF YOU CONSIDER IT A SIGN OF GETTING OLD, YOU NEED TO CHANGE YOUR ATTITUDE.
- NOT ALL HEARING AIDS ARE CREATED EQUAL. DECIDE WHICH OPTIONS YOU NEED THE MOST AND DISCUSS THEM WITH YOUR AUDIOLOGIST.

Then there is the cost of hearing aids, which can be an eye-opener. I saw some that cost under a thousand dollars, while others cost as much as eight thousand. I didn't completely "cheap out," but I did try to keep the price under three thousand dollars. I'm starting to believe my mother's favorite adage: Buy cheap—get cheap. My next pair (and there will be a next pair because nothing lasts forever) will probably have me eating Ramen Noodles for years. You get what you pay for. And while no hearing aid will ever restore your hearing to what it once was, the higher-priced units utilize the latest technologies and (I'm hoping) more natural sound. Herzfeld says she considers features that add to the cost: "financial-based needs."

My family has taken dealing with my hearing impairment one step further. My nephew is learning sign language. Every time I see him, he tries to teach me a little more of what he's learned. Too bad my memory is worse than my hearing. I may be doomed to a future of sibilance and loud background noise or leaving my hearing aids out and smiling politely at people while nodding, even when they are cursing me out.

Being hard of hearing made Ursula every
pharmacy customer's worst nightmare.

WITHIN EARSHOT
by Melanie Herzfeld, Au.D.

Hearing loss comes from a variety of causes, not just aging. My patients range in age from zero to 102. Some became hearing impaired through such things as medications, drugs, genetics, accidents, noise, disease, or aging. So, while some people think it is because of age, it does not have to be a sign of getting old. That said, as we age, things tend not to work quite the same as when we were younger. So, we have to accept hearing loss as a part of that, too.

The symptoms of hearing loss can be a clogged sensation, which is typical for wax, fluid in the middle ear, an external otitis or swimmer's ear, allergies or sinus issues. It can be a muffling of sounds, which is typically due to not hearing specific frequencies as well. It can be due to mishearing—again due to missing certain frequencies. It can also be a perception problem, not a peripheral hearing loss, but a central one. In this instance, such things as competing sounds, accents, and timing can interfere with understanding. Typically, as one ages, the hearing loss is best described as "spousal deafness" in that when one is at work, one will work harder to understand what is being said. But when one comes home, sits down to read the paper while watching television with the spouse in the kitchen running water, that person cannot hear the spouse well. Thus, the coined phrase "spousal deafness," which really means the beginning of hearing loss.

The difference between hearing loss in children and in adults has to do more with things like closure and timing issues versus language learning issues. As we age, our timing needs increase. It takes longer to fill in the blanks. For the young child or infant with hearing loss, the issues revolve around learning language. For the older adult the issues revolve around processing the language already learned.

Choosing an audiologist is really person specific. I like to think my patients enjoy coming to see me and value my opinion, but I also need to let them be the owner of their hearing loss. I can explain an audiogram, discuss its general implications, talk about amplification, but I do not have the hearing loss. So, I need to empower my patients. My famous "Bernie" story exemplifies this. I told a patient, a longstanding hearing aid user in his forties, that he would love the brand new digital aids. We made him up a pair of canal aids. Thirty days later, he met me in the hallway at the multi-specialty medical group where I was employed, grabbed my hand, and said, "Melanie, I love you, you are a great person, a great audiologist, but these hearing aids suck!" I realized I had predicted that he would love those aids. My advisor at the time said, "Since when do you own his loss?" I remember running back into the clinic and declaring that we will never again tell a patient what to try, only guide him or her in the process. So, to me, a good audiologist offers choices, allows patients to compare and contrast devices, tries a bunch of them on patients, and explains the differences.

Bells and whistles are not really necessarily bells and whistles but necessary add-ons. Does everyone need Bluetooth connectivity? That is a bell and whistle. Do you need an FM, a device which allows you to place a mic elsewhere and hear the lecturer directly in your aids? Again, a bell and whistle. But within the devices, the features that add to the cost I consider financial-based needs. The more bands for example, the more natural the sound and the better we are able to fine tune so that speech in noise is more comfortable, or so that feedback management is improved. The speech processor may be improved in a more sophisticated device than in the entry-level type. These are some features that improve the quality of listening but do add to the cost.

The brain is a wonderful thing. Imagine anything else that size absorbing that much knowledge, allowing us to do so much. So, now imagine the layout in the brain; everything has a spot but everything wants more space. If you are not using a space, the next-door warriors will move in and change the focus of that spot. It is hard to reclaim. So, if you are not using your hearing mechanism as it was intended, it becomes increasingly difficult to reclaim it. We now know that use of amplification for hearing help should be done sooner rather than later!

Lastly, you should all remember it is not the ear that hears. Simply put, it is the brain. And the more we tantalize the brain, support it, enhance its learning, the better off we are.

I hadn't really noticed that I had a hearing problem I just thought most people had given up speaking clearly.
—Hal Linden

C'MON NOW TOUCH ME BABY

In her book, *The Blind Assassin,* author Margaret Atwood wrote, "Touch comes before sight, before speech. It is the first language and the last, and it always tells the truth."

The sense of touch tells us so much. The softness of a baby's skin, the pain of injury, how tight our waistband feels when we eat too much. Heat, cold, and pressure are all part of touch—and the information we gather from that sensation can alert us to problems. Ever sit in a freezing-cold restaurant and wonder why they have the air-conditioning on in winter. It's our sense of touch that's telling us it's cold.

We don't only rely on the nerve endings in our skin to alert our touch sensors. Our muscles, joints, and internal organs detect touch as well. So, when something swells up that's not supposed to, the surrounding sensors send a signal to the brain that something is wrong.

Here's the good news: As you get older you will feel pain less.
Here's the bad news: As you get older, you will feel pain less. It's one of life's little ironies.

Experts blame the loss on less blood flowing to our spinal cords and brains. According to the National Institute of Health (NIH), diseases like nerve damage or diabetes could make the problem worse. If we can't differentiate between heat and cold like we used to, we risk hypothermia or heat stroke. That's why older people are always advised not to go outdoors during a heat wave, but to seek refuge instead in a cool place like their home, a mall, or movie theater. You may not feel the heat, but your organs will react to it all the same—and not in a good way.

According to experts, our blood vessels also lose elasticity as we get older, causing a decrease in circulation. That could make our metabolic response to cold slow down. Our brains may be shouting, "Conserve the heat!" but our blood vessels may be slow to react.

People who can't sense pressure also have an increased risk of falling. We've all heard that line from a commercial, "I've fallen and I can't get up." That happens when our feet can't feel the floor and we lose our orientation.

Our skin becomes thinner, dryer, and loses elasticity as we age. We produce less collagen and elastin. Doctors say changes in the touch sensation can also be caused by medications, nutrition problems, and nerve damage from diseases like diabetes.

Plus our cells may not be regenerating. Unfortunately, experts say cells that die because of aging are not replaced, and that such loss can impair organ function. Even worse, it could have a domino effect on other organs in the body. So, it's important to keep track of small changes in our health and discuss them with our physicians.

> *Where the senses fail us,*
> *reason must step in.*
> —Galileo Galilei

EXPERTS SAY:

- SEE A DOCTOR IF YOU FEEL UNSTEADY ON YOUR FEET.
- STAY INSIDE DURING TEMPERATURE EXTREMES.
- MAKE SURE YOUR HOT WATER HEATER IS SET TO LESS THAN 125 DEGREES TO ENSURE THE WATER COMING OUT OF THE TAP IS NOT SCALDING.
- AND WHEN OTHER PEOPLE TALK ABOUT IT BEING TOO HOT OR TOO COLD, HEED THEIR WARNINGS BECAUSE YOUR INTERNAL THERMOSTAT MAY NOT BE WORKING CORRECTLY. OR MAYBE THEIRS ISN'T. BUT AT LEAST IT WILL MAKE YOU AWARE OF A POTENTIAL PROBLEM.
- THERE IS A SILVER LINING ACCORDING TO SOME MEDICAL EXPERTS. COLDER TEMPERATURES MAY STIMULATE THE PRODUCTION OF BROWN FAT, WHICH KEEPS US WARM AND BURNS MORE CALORIES. IT'S NOT A GOOD REASON TO SHIVER, BUT IF YOU DON'T HAVE A SWEATER HANDY, IT MAY HELP YOU GET THROUGH A TEMPORARY CHILL.

" I DON'T THINK OF MY SKIN
AS SAGGY...I THINK OF IT
AS RELAXED-FIT!"

SKIN DEEP

Did I ever think that as I aged my legs would one-day resemble a roadmap? My veins, both thick and thin, travel down and around my limbs making them look like highways and small back streets. The bruises, scratches, and bumps that complete the twisting roadway represent outlying towns and pit stops. My favorite liver spot is a diner.

I don't feel old and, for sure, don't act old, but that's not what the mirror says or what other people see. Fine lines, smile lines, brown spots, crow's feet, and skin tags have replaced a firm face and clear complexion. Plus, other skin irritants, like itching.

Despite thinking I did everything humanly possible for my skin, I must say that looking in the mirror provides no payoff. But perhaps it's because I didn't know then what I know now.

I never really gave much thought to my skin in my younger days. I never thought about staying out of the sun and using moisturizers, retinols, and what have you. But with aging comes a whole new set of dos and don'ts.

Now I DO use sunscreen. When I'm at the beach I DO sit under an umbrella. I DO try to eat the right foods. I DO use moisturizers. I DO exercise. And I DO try to get enough sleep.

I DON'T smoke. I DON'T use soap on my face because it's drying. And whether or not I drink too much depends on the evening.

I am a five-foot-three woman in search of much needed but lost elastin and collagen—a woman who knows that trying to defy gravity is a lost cause. So, I do what I can and hope for the best.

DERMATOLOGIST CLIFFORD BERCK SAYS:

- HAVING A FACIAL EVERY SO OFTEN DEFINITELY HELPS. IT CLEANS THE SKIN; IT GETS RID OF THE DEAD CELLS; IT MOISTURIZES AND PLUMPS IT UP.
- TRY TO STAY UPBEAT BECAUSE FROWNING AND STRESS CAUSE WRINKLES.
- STAY OUT OF THE SUN. IT IS A NUCLEAR REACTOR. IF YOU NEED VITAMIN D, TAKE A SUPPLEMENT.
- USE MILD CLEANSERS AND INCREASE THE USE OF MOISTURIZERS WITH A MINIMUM SPF OF THIRTY.
- LIMIT ALCOHOL.
- THE USE OF RETINOIDS SHOULD ONLY BE PRESCRIBED BY YOUR DERMATOLOGIST BECAUSE EACH INDIVIDUAL'S SKIN TYPE AND TOLERANCE VARIES.

Also, self-tanners help reduce the appearance of varicose and spider veins on your legs. And you could also wear support hose.

Even though we can't be in complete control of risk factors that negatively impact our skin, we are in control of our behavior.

So, behave yourself.

Wear a smile and have friends;
wear a scowl and have wrinkles.
—George Eliot

MOUTHING
OFF

EAT THIS!

If I hear one more person, read one more article, or see another commercial on what we should and shouldn't eat, I am going to throw myself against the wall. Every day there is a new food. Every day there is a new theory. A news breaking discovery. What was gospel last year is now shredded wheat and relegated to the garbage.

Oh, and by the way, wheat is considered by some an unhealthy, allergic food. *Just saying.*

There are diets on how to live longer, how to be healthy, what supplements to take, and what supplements not to take. There's how you can have younger-looking skin, how to not lose your memory, how to be skinny in thirty minutes, and how to have gorgeous hair. How to. How to. How to. No matter how old you are, it's a battle trying to keep up.

But there is one thing everyone can agree on: Eating well is important.

It is key to keeping our immune system strong, which enables us to fight off disease, quickens our recuperation time, maintains our mental acuity, and helps us better-manage chronic health problems.

But our nutritional journey is a challenging road to navigate as we age. Remember the days when you could touch your toes, or walk for long periods of time without huffing and puffing? Well, all that's changed. Our metabolism slows down, too. So, it is important to be as active as we can be. Physical activity helps maintain a healthy body weight and contributes to a better quality of life.

Experts say that beginning in our fifties and thereafter we require fewer calories. Which boils down to this: Eat less but eat more nutritionally rich foods like fruits, vegetables, nuts, fish, and whole grains. Limit your intake of sugar, salt, bad carbs—like refined flour—and use only heart healthy fats. And don't forget to drink water. Water is essential in keeping us hydrated. It regulates our body fluids. And if you find drinking water a chore, as many people do, fill up a large container of the liquid and sip it throughout the day. Never underestimate the value of water. It helps our kidneys function properly and reduces problems of constipation.

Also on the table for discussion is whether or not we should take supplements. Most health professionals I have spoken with say it is healthier to get our vitamins and minerals from whole foods that are natural. Supplements give you only part of a whole and they are manufactured with other ingredients. While supplements can be helpful and part of your daily regimen, you should contact your health care provider to see if they are right for you. As Hippocrates, the father of medicine said, "Let food be thy medicine and medicine be thy food."

If you have specific health concerns, or if you just need help in making the right food choices, a nutritionist or registered dietician will be able to help you with specific diet guidelines based on your history.

NUTRITIONIST MARNIE SCHEFTER SAYS:

- LOSING WEIGHT BECOMES MORE DIFFICULT AS WE AGE BECAUSE OUR METABOLISM SLOWS DOWN.
- TOO MUCH SALT CAN LEAD TO BLOATING. KEEP SODIUM INTAKE FROM 1,000 TO 2,000 MG A DAY.
- HEARTBURN AND REFLUX ARE CAUSED BY HIGH FAT. AVOID SPICY FOODS, FRIED FOODS, DAIRY PRODUCTS, CREAM SAUCES, FATTY DRESSINGS, AND FOODS THAT ARE HIGH IN ACID.
- ADDING FIBER HELPS KEEP FOOD MOVING IN THE RIGHT DIRECTION.

The older you get, the tougher it is to lose weight, because by then your body and your fat are really good friends.
—Bob Hope

I'VE ALWAYS WANTED DIMPLES—BUT NOT THIS MANY

Show me a woman who has never been concerned about diet and exercise and I will show you a liar! Face it, D & E are as American as baseball and apple pie (not to be confused with strudel, which is, of course, imported).

If any of the following diets sound familiar, raise your hand, unless you have arthritis, in which case, whistle. "You do know how to whistle, don't you? You just put your lips together and blow!" Extra credit if you remember what film that is from and how svelte the actress who said it was. I'm pretty sure she thought about diet and exercise. A lot.

Do any of these diets ring a bell?
AYDS (an unfortunate name)
3-Hour Diet
Atkins Diet
Beverly Hills Diet
Blood-type Diet
Cabbage Soup Diet (especially aromatic)
Diet Center Diet

Drinking Man's Diet
Dukan Diet
Glycemic Index Diet
Grapefruit Diet
Jenny Craig
Macrobiotic Diet
Master Cleanse
Medifast
Metracal (Yeah. We're going back into the archives)
Nutrisystem
Optifast
Pritikin Diet
Scarsdale Diet
Seafood Diet (reminds me of the old joke: I'm on a seafood diet. I see food, I eat it.)
Slimfast
South Beach Diet
Stillman Diet
Weight Watchers
Zone Diet

So, what's the problem? We feel deprived, so we eat. Then we become depressed because we ate. Then we throw ourselves under the bus and say we'll start tomorrow (famous last words).

This is something that affects all ages, so why are we talking about it in *Over-Sixty Shades of Gray?* Because our size increases with age. Losing weight becomes more difficult as we get older. The young at heart have to work twice as hard at diet and exercise to get half the results that younger people achieve. Our metabolism slows down with each new year, so even though we try harder, we see less results, not to mention, we may care less about what we eat. Plus, we are losing muscle tone. Our once youthful six-pack typically turns to flab by age seventy. When muscle goes away, fat steps in to take its place. We can blame burning fewer calories on hormones—just like we do for practically everything else covered in this book. Instead of *Over-Sixty Shades of Gray*, we could have called it *For Whom the Hor-Moans.*

HERE IS A CROSS-SECTION OF HELPFUL EXERCISES TO CONSIDER:

- WALKING. MOST EVERYBODY DOES IT. EVEN THOUGH IT'S A WEIGHT-BEARING EXERCISE, IT'S NOT STRENUOUS AND YOU CAN MOVE AT YOUR OWN PACE.
- YOGA. I'LL BE THE FIRST TO ADMIT I HATE THE STILLNESS OF YOGA, BUT EVEN I KNOW IT'S BENEFICIAL. AND YOU MAY LOVE IT. YOU DON'T HAVE TO TWIST LIKE A PRETZEL. JUST DO THE EASY MOVES TO STRETCH OUT AND INCREASE BALANCE AND FLEXIBILITY. YOGA OFFERS A MULTITUDE OF BENEFITS.
- DANCING. YOU CAN DO IT ALL ALONE. YOU CAN DO IT WITH A FRIEND OR LOVED ONE. I USED TO DANCE AROUND THE HOUSE WITH MY PARROT. HE LOVED IT. UNFORTUNATELY, I DID ALL THE MOVING AND HE JUST SAT ON MY HAND. GUESS THAT'S WHY HE'S DEAD AND I'M NOT. *JUST SAYING.*

SO, WHAT CAN MEN AND WOMEN DO TO HELP WARD OFF EXCESS BAGGAGE?

- EAT MORE SALADS AND LEAN PROTEIN.
- WHEN YOU CRAVE A SWEET, EAT FRUIT FIRST.
- STAY AWAY FROM BAD CARBS. THEY INCREASE YOUR APPETITE.
- STAY WELL HYDRATED. SOMETIMES WHEN WE FEEL HUNGRY, WE'RE REALLY ONLY THIRSTY.
- AND MOVE, STRETCH, ENGAGE, AND ENJOY.

We can't recapture our youth. I tried chasing mine down the block and got winded. So, we have to learn to make healthy choices and try to accept our bodies.

"I used to eat a lot of natural foods until I learned that most people die of natural causes."
— Author Unknown.

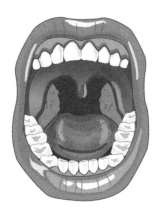

DO YOU HAVE A FOUL MOUTH?

I'm not talking about language that would make a sailor blush. I'm talking about inflamed gums and loose or missing teeth.

Many of the changes that happen with aging are beyond our control. Losing our teeth isn't one of them. Most tooth loss is caused by either periodontal disease coupled with bone loss—which is preventable—or trauma. If you have ever looked at hockey players coming off the ice, you'll know what I mean by trauma. An accident, sports, or a barroom brawl can contribute to tooth loss. Getting older just means we have had more opportunities during our lifetimes to suffer dental damage.

So, let's talk gum disease. There's a line at the end of the 1992 movie *Prelude to a Kiss*, starring Meg Ryan and Alec Baldwin, where the old man says: "Can I give you two a piece of advice? Floss." That pretty much sums it up. If you take good care of your choppers, they should still be around to take care of you. I say "should" because some people develop periodontal problems because of systemic disease or medications they take. According to Dr. Elliot Auerbach, "Bone loss from periodontal disease produces a widespread pattern of gum and bone loss around a tooth or group of teeth. He says gums are normally supported by, and receive some of their blood supply from, underlying bone. As bone is lost from periodontal inflammation, the overlying gum may recede." The problem is, once you've suffered bone deterioration, your teeth loosen and are prone to accidental loss.

I had loose front teeth because of periodontal problems. Then, I needed an unrelated operation. When they inserted a breathing tube to feed oxygen to my lungs the tube pushed my two front teeth all the way out. It was my hillbilly look. And for years after that, I had a removable bridge. Those were miserable years.

Dr. Auerbach says, "Denture wearers are not excluded from problems, either. They may suffer from difficulty in chewing, recurrent mouth sores, and chronic irritation at the corners of the mouth."

I only found satisfaction after I got implants to replace the teeth I lost. People who have implants told me they feel natural—like your own teeth—and I didn't believe them. But it's true. They feel like the teeth I was born with, except I didn't have teeth when I was born.

And if you haven't figured it out by now—because it seems like it's a running theme in every chapter—hormonal changes can play a part. "[Dry mouth] and burning sensations in the lips, tongue, and gums may be side effects resulting from sensitivity to mouthwashes and toothpastes, certain medications, chemotherapy, and radiation treatment; in some cases, no definite cause can be determined."

If people wrinkle their noses when you begin to speak, you might be the victim of bad breath. It could be caused by sinus infections, high blood sugar, or tongue plaque. However, if you drink a lot of coffee, eat a lot of garlic, or smoke, you could be the cause of your problem. I have a friend who always says chewing coffee beans and eating parsley help minimize foul breath.

Still, the general consensus is, we are responsible for the condition of our teeth, so even though there might be mitigating circumstances, our mouths are what we have made them.

PERIODONTIST ELLIOTT AUERBACH SAYS:

- THERE IS A STRONG CORRELATION BETWEEN AGE AND ORAL CANCERS (TONGUE, LIP, FLOOR OF THE MOUTH, PALATE).
- ALCOHOL AND TOBACCO CAN INCREASE THE INCIDENCE OF ORAL CANCERS.
- LIMIT THE INTAKE OF SUGAR, WHICH CONTRIBUTES TO THE DEVELOPMENT OF PLAQUE.
- IT'S IMPORTANT TO SEE YOUR DENTIST AT LEAST ONCE A YEAR FOR A CLEANING. IT'S THE MOST EFFECTIVE WAY TO MAINTAIN A HEALTHY MOUTH.

If the expense of dental work is holding you back, I would just like to add one more thought. Back in the day, when I was young and nubile, I worked as a dental assistant. I saw people with really bad teeth almost every day. And when my employer explained to some patients they would need extensive crown and bridge work, or dentures, or whatever, they often balked at the price. But as he would put it: "You'd pay more than that for a car that you may use once or twice a day and may last five or ten years. Why wouldn't you pay that much for teeth that you'll use more than three times a day and hope will last a lifetime?" *Just saying.*

DIGESTIVE
DISSONANCE

Essay No. 22

BATHROOM BLUES

If the problem of I-R-R-E-G-U-L-A-R-I-T-Y has you down in the dumps, you are not alone.

An estimated 42 million people in the United States have experienced the discomfort and frustration of constipation. I'm one of them. So is my husband. As we age, feeling relieved is often the highlight of our days. I think it's one of the best feelings in the world. Really, I do. Or I do-do.

Take the aging population as an example. Most of us are under the impression that constipation comes with the territory. That's only partially true, but it's not a direct result of aging. What plays an important role in this particular age group is the continued use of medications, which many adults over sixty-five take. There are other contributing factors to the risk of constipation: low-fiber diet, reduced fluid intake, inactivity, and ignoring the urge to go to the bathroom.

But what actually is constipation? According to the National Digestive

Disease Information Clearing House, "Constipation is a very common condition in which a person has fewer than three bowel movements a week," or hard, dry poop. Constipation may last a day or two, or it can be chronic and last for months, even years. Although it can be severe, experts say constipation is not dangerous. It just puts you in a lousy mood.

Ask my husband. He complains if he misses one bowel movement. I'm sure if you ask your friends, they will tell you how not being able to go to the bathroom is a miserable feeling. We can feel bloated, experience pains in our abdomen, and develop hemorrhoids just from trying to squeeze out a little relief. It can ruin our day. Now that is a real pain in the ass! There have been so many times I have been constipated where, had I squeezed any harder, I would have hemorrhaged. And the only thing I had to show for it was hemorrhoids.

Since treatment depends on the cause, severity, and duration of the problem, it is important for people to keep in mind not to self-medicate. And continued use of laxatives can cause dependency while offering little relief. So, getting the proper diagnosis from your health care provider is important.

REGISTERED DIETICIAN MARNI SCHEFTER RECOMMENDS:

- INCREASING PHYSICAL ACTIVITY.
- EATING PLENTY OF FRUITS, VEGETABLES, AND GRAINS AND IF THAT DOESN'T WORK, SUPPLEMENTING YOUR DIET WITH BULK-FORMING AGENTS (MORE FIBER).
- DRINKING PLENTY OF WATER.

Also, try a stool softener, or acupuncture for increased motility. Remember, if you need to change your medication, do so under a doctor's care.

It doesn't hurt to have a hot cup of coffee or tea in the morning to help get things moving.

And never ignore the urge to go.

> *When God closes a door, he opens a window. Sounds to me like he's on the toilet.*
> —Dana Gould

YOUR COMING OUT PARTY: SOLIDS, LIQUIDS, GAS

The battle against aging is a losing proposition. We lose our fight against gravity. We lose our fight with hormones. Our collagen abandons us. And what are we left with? Burping, spitting, and farting—not necessarily in that order. And if your nose is like mine: You think it's mucus, but it's (s)not—or as I like to call it, *sticky snot*. I think my nasal mucus is growing agoraphobic in old age. It doesn't want to leave my nose. But we'll get to that later.

First up, burping. Everybody does it. In some countries, it's considered a compliment. Babies are encouraged to do it. So, why does it seem so unseemly when an older person belches in public? Okay. Maybe they are not the delicate burps of our youth. For some reason the older we get, the more intensely trapped gas strives to exit our bodies. As my uncle used to say, "If you were stuck in there, you'd want to get out, too." Don't sweat it.

We are encouraged to burp from infancy. Everybody gets air trapped in their abdomen from eating, chewing, swallowing, and drinking carbonated beverages. Like cream, trapped air wants to rise to the top and exit out our mouths. Better that than burping out of our noses or our ears. Although, if we burped out of our noses, it might expel some of that sticky snot I was talking about.

The good news is that the food that causes belching hasn't had a chance to decompose, so it doesn't smell really bad. If it does, see your doctor. You may have an infection or obstruction. Or, it may be you are consuming foods with a high-sulfur content.

When the gas erupts below the belt, things get dicier. Digestive enzymes have had a chance to kick in and break down foods, causing more of an aroma. So, let's talk flatulence. Everyone farts. *SeniorHealth364.com* says most people pass gas ten to twenty times a day. Some people just let it rip. Others try to disguise it by making some other noise. Then there are the suppressors. When I first met my husband, I refused to fart in his presence for the first five years of our marriage. He had no such tendencies. After five years, I decided it was time to switch to an eye for an eye—or fart for a fart—approach. One of my relatives refers to the passing of gas as "resonating." It sounds more distinguished that way. More musical. But gas is gas and, as we get older, the *great gas crisis* plagues us more often. We blame it on beans, or wheat, or claim we have a sensitivity to gluten. It may be all of the above. Or it may just be that we are getting older. Sometimes, we develop an intolerance for foods we freely ate when we were younger. I can no longer eat nuts. My husband had to give up onions. Bowel muscles, which weaken with age, make it more difficult to hold back everything that wants out. And let's talk about the high-fiber diets that everyone tells us are so important. Yes, high fiber helps the gastrointestinal system, but it's another cause of flatulence. It's not true that all fiber is indigestible. According to *MedicineNet.com*, your colon is capable of digesting fiber "to a small extent" and the resulting bacteria produces gas. Unfortunately, the foods that can be broken down—and the amount of gas produced—varies from person to person, so there's not a lot we can do about it. The benefit of eating fiber far outweighs the embarrassment of farting.

EXPERTS SAY:

- ELIMINATE STARCHY FOODS LIKE POTATOES, CORN, BEANS, AND CARBONATED BEVERAGES.
- CARBOHYDRATES CREATE FLATULENCE WHEN THEY BREAK DOWN, SO IF YOU ARE GOING TO EAT THEM, STICK TO COMPLEX CARBS LIKE FRUITS AND VEGETABLES. SAY NO TO PROCESSED CARBS.
- CUT DOWN THE NUMBER OF CRUCIFEROUS VEGGIES YOU EAT, LIKE BROCCOLI, CAULIFLOWER, AND CABBAGE, BUT DON'T ELIMINATE THEM BECAUSE THEY ARE STILL GOOD FOR YOU.
- WATCH YOUR INTAKE OF DAIRY AND PROTEINS, LIKE EGGS, WHICH CAN ALSO CONTRIBUTE TO GAS.

Other helpful tips: Use a probiotic, take a digestive enzyme supplement, chew s-l-o-w-l-y, and stop smoking so you are not sucking in excess air with every puff.

Now let's talk about spitting and drooling. I mean, everybody spits. If you have ever sat in the front row of a theater when a musical is playing, you know what it's like to be showered by someone's DNA. We all spray a little saliva, whether talking, sneezing, or coughing, but it seems to be more noticeable as we get older.

The simplest ways to prevent spitting is by swallowing more often, having dental problems corrected, and/or asking your doctor about medications that can reduce secretions.

Dr. Elliot Auerbach says there are many reasons for increased spitting:

- Difficulty swallowing saliva or foods, which could be a side effect of certain medications.
- Undiagnosed or untreated gastro-esophageal reflux.
- Dry mouth associated with decreased salivary flow.
- Excessive nasal or sinus secretions.
- Depression.
- Alzheimer's disease, dementia.

Finally, let's talk about my all-time favorite secretion: *sticky snot*. Yes, we all blow our noses, but as we get older, our mucus gains the resilience that our skin loses. But there are simple treatments. Steam, whether from a shower or just washing dishes, does a lot to loosen up the mucus in our nasal passages and sinuses. In the absence of steam, there's always saline nose spray. It goes a long way in aiding the eviction of uninvited guests and helps you breathe easier.

A FART IS JUST YOUR ARSE APPLAUDING.
— BILLY CONOLLY

Essay No. 24

"It makes you look fifty years younger."

FROM PAMPERS TO DEPENDS:
OR WHY YOU SHOULDN'T EAT THE YELLOW SNOW

It's harder to be anal retentive when you are older. Literally. Just like other muscles that aren't as springy as they were in our youth, neither is the sphincter, and this could result in fecal incontinence. The front is no better. Doctors say bladder muscles weaken as we age for varying reasons and the phrase "peed in our pants" is no longer just a reaction to something funny or scary. Like infants coming into this world, we oftentimes need protection for what we can't control.

First the facts: The National Association for Continence says 25 million people in North America suffer from incontinence or, more simply stated, a loss of bowel or bladder control. It may just be a few drops, or a gusher, but either way, when it lets loose unexpectedly, it can be embarrassing.

According to urologist Dr. Jessica Kreshover, urinary incontinence is more common in women than men because the former have babies. She says pregnancy, childbirth, and menopause weaken the muscles we need to hold urine in the bladder. And while loss of bladder control may be more common in elderly women, the National Association for Continence says one in five adults over forty suffer from incontinence. So, don't let those forty and fifty-year-olds give you any holier-than-thou attitude. They're apt to leak one day, too.

With men, the National Institute of Health (NIH) says urinary incontinence is more likely caused by prostate blockage. If men can't pee when they feel the urge, experts say their bladders become overfilled and leak when they least expect it.

The list of causes continues. Experts from the Mayo Clinic say pelvic injuries, nerve damage from diseases like diabetes, MS, Parkinson's, or even arthritis can play a part in the inability to stay dry. People with arthritis may have difficulty undressing in time. Any illness or medication that slows you down or has loss-of-control as a side effect can contribute to incontinence.

But it's more complex than that because there are different types of urinary incontinence. Doctors say stress incontinence is caused by pressure on the bladder and could be triggered by coughing, sneezing, or laughing. This type of incontinence is often caused by pregnancy—so, blame your kids! Stress incontinence can also be caused by cancer treatments or prostate surgery.

Overflow incontinence is the result of an overly full bladder from an enlarged prostate or anything else that might block the urethra. According to doctors, constipation or nerve damage from a stroke or diabetes can be contributing factors. Involuntary contractions of the bladder may cause urge incontinence, which could be the result of disease, injury, or pelvic floor atrophy. And functional incontinence happens when something prevents you from getting to the bathroom in time, like a bad hip or the inability to walk.

While we are on the subject, let's talk about urinary tract infections, or UTIs. I am the queen of UTIs. They are bacterial infections notable for increasing your urge to pee, only to reward you with pain when you empty your bladder. UTIs are usually treated with antibiotics.

However, Dr. Kreshover says your best defense against infection is to keep your liquids flowing. She says the more fluids that move through your system, the less likely you are to have bacteria build-up. A sparkling river is better than a stagnant pool. So, drink lots of water.

Fecal incontinence is less common. According to Medtronic, one in ten adults may suffer from fecal incontinence, although experts advise it's *not* a normal part of aging. Doctors blame it on nerve or muscle damage and, in some cases, damage caused by surgery. Conditions like diarrhea, constipation, or irritable bowel syndrome can also cause this type of incontinence. Other causes include rectal prolapse, childbirth, and inactivity.

If you suffer from any kind of incontinence, there are several things you can do about it.

FIRST AND FOREMOST, SEE A PHYSICIAN, WHO MAY RECOMMEND:

- DRINKING PLENTY OF WATER TO TREAT FECAL INCONTINENCE. AVOID CAFFEINE, ALCOHOL, MILK, AND CARBONATED BEVERAGES.
- BULK LAXATIVES OR ANTI-DIARRHEAL MEDICATIONS.
- ADDING MORE FIBER TO YOUR DIET IN THE FORM OF FRUITS, VEGETABLES, AND WHOLE GRAINS.
- TRAINING YOURSELF TO HAVE REGULAR BOWEL MOVEMENTS TO PREVENT CONSTIPATION.

WAYS TO TREAT LEAKY VALVES:

- URGE INCONTINENCE CAN SOMETIMES BE TREATED WITH MEDICATION.
- STRESS INCONTINENCE CAN BE TREATED SURGICALLY.
- OTHER TREATMENTS INCLUDE BEHAVIORAL TRAINING, PELVIC FLOOR MUSCLE EXERCISES, FLUID AND DIET MANAGEMENT, SCHEDULED BATHROOM TRIPS, HORMONE REPLACEMENT, MEDICAL DEVICES, OR BIOFEEDBACK.

Physicians we have spoken with say people sometimes feel embarrassed discussing something as personal as incontinence, but it's important to remember that your physician sees this every day.

Incontinence can be managed.

To pee, or not to pee, that is the question.
—A Little Bit Shakespeare

PISSED OFF!

A couple of days ago, at six in the morning, my husband called me into the bathroom because he wanted me to see he was peeing in two different directions. So, I watched him. And he peed for a l-o-o-o-n-g time. There was a stream going to the back of the bowl and another stream going to the front of the bowl. It looked like a perfect V. I told him his penis was bipolar, but he insisted it has a split personality.

After his exam at the urologist's office a couple of weeks later, my husband was told his prostate was a little enlarged. But everything else was within normal limits. That's a very good thing.

Although urologists treat both sexes for conditions and diseases, I guess you could say they are to men what gynecologists are to women.

Women go to their doctors with a slew of questions. Men, not so much.

In the past I would accompany my husband to all of his doctor appointments and ask the questions he wouldn't think to ask. Like most of us, he just wants to know he's okay.

UROLOGIST JESSICA KRESHOVER SAYS:

- PROSTATE ENLARGEMENT IS ONE OF THE BIGGEST CONTRIBUTORS TO URINARY FREQUENCY.
- LIMIT THE USE OF CAFFEINE AND ALCOHOL TO REDUCE THE INCIDENCE OF KIDNEY STONES AND URINARY FREQUENCY.
- PENISES DON'T SHRINK AS MEN AGE. IT JUST LOOKS THAT WAY BECAUSE OF WEIGHT GAIN.

Like the saying goes: "Knowledge is power."

The greatness of a man is only measured by his urologist. —Bob Saget

NOT DONE YET

"It's arthritis. Probably caused from clinging to life."

ARTHUR ITIS IS NOT MY FRIEND

My grandfather often said, "After sixty, you get a new pain every day." Papa's saying was so memorable, everyone in my family quotes it. He earned his living as a bricklayer, including work on the Empire State Building, and accumulated a fair share of work-related pains over the years. When he spoke of "a new pain every day," he was probably talking about rheumatic pain and arthritis—or as he called it "Arthur Itis." I'm sure digestive problems, foot pain, and a whole host of minor ailments helped fill in the gaps. My grandfather knew what he was talking about. According to the Centers for Disease Control (CDC), the risk of developing arthritis increases with age. And ladies, watch out, because six out of ten arthritis sufferers will be women (yet we live longer—try figuring that one out). Anyway, that statistic doesn't give us a lot to look forward to. So, what can we do about it?

The word "arthritis" most commonly refers to inflamed joints and is often used to describe autoimmune diseases like osteoarthritis, rheumatoid arthritis, systemic lupus, fibromyalgia, and gout. Because it covers a host of ailments, symptoms vary, but most commonly involve joint pain and/or stiffness. And there are many factors that may contribute to the cause of our pain, like excess weight, joint damage from injuries, microbial infections, or repetitive stress.

YOU MAY BE ABLE TO MINIMIZE THE PAIN BY IMPROVING YOUR QUALITY OF LIFE:

- EAT PROPERLY. THE ARTHRITIS FOUNDATION RECOMMENDS A MEDITERRANEAN DIET THAT IS HIGH IN FRUITS, VEGETABLES, FISH, NUTS, AND BEANS, AND LOW IN PROCESSED FOODS AND SATURATED FATS.
- REDUCE WEIGHT. THE CDC SAYS LOSING JUST 5 PERCENT OF EXCESS WEIGHT CAN REDUCE PAIN AND DISABILITY.
- EXERCISE. WHETHER IT'S AQUATIC, LOW IMPACT, YOGA (GOD, HOW I HATE YOGA), STRETCHING, BIKING, DANCING AROUND THE HOUSE, OR SIMPLY CLEANING IT—MOVE—BUT DON'T OVERDO IT. DOCTORS SAY EVEN SMALL RANGE OF MOTION EXERCISE CAN HELP SOMEONE WITH SEVERE ARTHRITIC PAIN. EVERYONE IS DIFFERENT. EXERCISE MIGHT HURT IN THE BEGINNING (AND WHO WANTS TO EXERCISE WHEN THEY ARE IN PAIN), BUT YOU HAVE TO START SOMEWHERE. DISCUSS WITH YOUR DOCTOR HOW MUCH MOVEMENT WOULD BE BENEFICIAL FOR YOU. REMEMBER, YOU ARE ONLY HURTING YOURSELF WHEN YOU MAKE EXCUSES.
- ACUPUNCTURE. ONCE YOU GET PAST THE IDEA OF SOMEONE STICKING YOU FULL OF PINS LIKE A VOODOO DOLL, YOU MAY FIND THAT ACUPUNCTURE PROVIDES TREMENDOUS RELIEF. I WAS ALWAYS A SKEPTIC BUT RESORTED TO IT ON A CRUISE AFTER I HURT MY BACK. IT DID WONDERS FOR ME AND SAVED MY VACATION.

If a change in diet and exercise doesn't work for you, your doctor may recommend medication, occupational therapy, splints, or even surgery. Once again, discuss your condition with your physician and see what he or she recommends.

> *"I don't deserve this award, but I have arthritis and I don't deserve that either."*
> —Jack Benny

I SHOULD HAVE BEEN A ROCKETTE

Nobody dances like me. I'm so good, I dance in my sleep. Come to think of it, I only dance in my sleep. And if I'm going to be truthful, I'm not really asleep at all, which is the problem. I'm trying to fall asleep but suffer from something called restless leg syndrome or RLS.

Considering how much I thrash about at night, I should be thin. Skinny, actually. There's a whole lot of calorie burning going on. Unfortunately, it doesn't work that way, although I have very slender ankles.

In retrospect, I should have been alerted to my propensity for RLS earlier in life. After all, I've always suffered from the what I like to call "knee hyper-bobbing." Actually, my knee isn't doing any of the work at all. It's my foot and ankle that are driving the hyper-bob motion, but they are both associated with my leg and restless. Sometimes I suffer from *double-hyper-bob*. That's when both knees dance at the same time, although not necessarily in unison. The gifted observer might recognize my dual RLS. The casual observer will only think I need to pee.

In my younger years, I could fall asleep anywhere, instantly. Not so much today. No at all today!

I've tried warm baths before bed. *Doesn't help.*
Botanical creams to calm my legs. *Doesn't help.*
Advil. *Doesn't help.*
Wine. *Doesn't help.*

Apparently, there is no cure for restless leg syndrome. I read where I may have an iron deficiency. I could take iron pills but they'll probably constipate me and, then, I won't be able to sleep. That's a no-win solution. I stopped smoking, only have a half cup of coffee a day, and exercise regularly. *Doesn't help.*

I've toyed with the idea of taking an antihistamine to make me drowsy. It's something to consider. And my nose won't run. I wonder if it lessens drooling?

But mostly I believe I'm doomed to RLS forever. My mother had it, as does my brother, although Mom no longer suffers from it. She's dead. And I haven't received any phone calls from the cemetery saying her coffin just went bouncing down the hill on its own power. So, there is a cure for RLS. Just not the one anyone wants.

"You know you're getting old when all the names in your black book have M.D. after them."
— Harrison Ford

TO SLEEP, PERCHANCE TO DREAM

How many of us complain about having a lousy night's sleep, if we were lucky enough to sleep at all? I'm certainly one of those people and so is my husband and many of my friends. Sleep problems in older adults are very common. According to the Center for Disease Control, 50 to 70 million people in the United States have chronic sleep problems and wakefulness. As we age our sleep patterns often change. Sometimes we become sleepier in the early evening and wake up earlier in the morning.

According to psychologist Dr. Ann Lane: "A majority of my patients of all ages complain of sleep issues. Chronic difficulties in falling asleep, staying asleep, and frequent wakefulness are especially common in older adults. Insufficient sleep causes daytime sleepiness and can affect memory, judgement, alertness, and mood. Daytime fatigue also places one at greater risk for an injury."

No matter your age, getting the right amount of sleep is important. Sleep is vital to not only our physical health but our emotional health as well. Think of all the times we had a bad night's sleep and felt cranky, sick, and didn't have that get-up-and-go feeling the following day. Experts agree that proper sleep allows us to avoid these bad feelings while repairing cell damage, improving memory function, and preventing disease. Like taking your temperature, physicians consider sleep to be a measure of a person's health. How much sleep one need depends on the individual. What's considered normal for some may not be normal for others.

But new research indicates that sleep does not change that much from the age of sixty on up. And if you are sleeping poorly, according Dr. Michael Vitelli, a sleep researcher and professor of psychiatry and behavioral sciences at the University of Washington, it has more to do with illness and medications. It seems obvious that the more problems an older adult has the worse he or she sleeps, which in my household is not necessarily the case. I don't have pain. I don't take medications, nor do I have health issues that haven't already been resolved. But let's first go back and try to understand why our sleep patterns change as we age. This exercise can help us fight the frustration of those endless nights.

Blame it on the growth hormones. A decreasing amount of melatonin makes us have more wakeful moments during the night. Or because of sleepiness during the day, you may feel the need to take a nap. How often have you heard a friend say, "I think I'll take melatonin?" Personally, I know a number of people who do just that.

Over-the-counter or prescribed medications may also be contributing factors to sleepless nights. According to Dr. Lane, other causes of insomnia include excessive caffeine, alcohol, pain, frequent urination, and mental health issues.

So, if sleep is problematic, it's important to identify why you can't sleep. Is it stress? Is it a health problem? Are you feeling depressed?

After giving these questions some thought, you may want to assess your diet, your sleep environment, or what you eat and drink before bedtime.

During the day, try to get more socially involved and make sure to get enough sunlight, which helps regulate melatonin.

Dr. Lane also suggests exercise earlier in the day. "I help people create a reasonable plan to establish sleep hygiene, but my primary goal is to help identify and work through the worries and stressors that haunt many seniors and keep them up at night."

ACCORDING TO THE NATIONAL SLEEP FOUNDATION:

- STICK TO A REGULAR BEDTIME.
- TURN OFF ALL COMPUTERS AND TELEVISIONS AT LEAST ONE HOUR BEFORE GOING TO BED.
- TAKE THE TIME TO RELAX BEFORE BEDTIME. TAKE A BATH. DO SOME DEEP BREATHING EXERCISES. HAVE A CUP OF DECAFFEINATED TEA. I LIKE CHAMOMILE.
- TRY NOT TO NAP DURING THE DAY.

Don't spend a lot of time in bed. Get out of bed if you can't fall asleep. Train your brain to understand that the bed is for sleeping only. Well, maybe not only sleeping...

If all else fails, see a professional.

SHRINK WRAPPED

Going to therapy for many years has given me the self-awareness to recognize when I am behaving like an asshole. Don't get me wrong. Therapy has changed my life. Prior to now, I was broken. I lived on a tightrope. I had very little, if any, self-respect. I was a hypochondriac. I had a doctor for every body part. I was funny and had a sense of humor, which sort of maintained what little balance I had. I was a mother of a young child and wanted to be a better mother to my child than my mother was to me. I was also a mad, angry housewife. These were just some of the things that catapulted me into therapy.

It was not an easy journey. At times, it was painful. At times, therapy was confusing. But most of the time, it was scary and unsettling. I would recognize some of my unattractive qualities and feel embarrassed to the point of wanting to hide.

Looking back at my relationship with my parents, for example, was frequently painful. What they said. How they said it. How they treated me. How I never measured up. I felt I was more of an intrusion than a blessing. I felt small. The result of all my experiences with them—

good and bad—defined me as the person I am today. Through my therapy, I learned about them. I learned how their behaviors toward me influenced my relationships and behaviors with others as well as myself. I learned about their shortcomings and what they were going through. I eventually came to understand that we all come from stuff. Our past relationships are a part of us and we learn HOW to deal.

It's never easy facing yourself in the mirror honestly. I was doing the work as best I could. In time, I began to see that proverbial light at the end of the tunnel. And I began to feel hopeful.

I knew I didn't like the now, but I was terrified of the future. Doing what I was doing wasn't doing it for me anymore, but I knew I had to hold on.

There are times in our lives when we may hit a wall. Sometimes we just need to bounce ideas and listen to suggestions that can help us in particular situations. Or try and understand why someone is pissing us off. After all, can we be totally objective about ourselves?

Whatever the reason there are always questions and—hopefully— answers not too far behind. And in searching for answers, I realized there is not just one perspective. There are many different types of therapies and different approaches to the way therapy is practiced. It's not a one-size-fits-all.

Dr. Ann Lane and Dr. Jerold Gold say:

- Try not to be stuck in the past with painful feelings.
- Mourning losses is an essential process of letting go and moving forward.
- Stay active and involved. Exercising, meditating, volunteering, and enjoying hobbies are ways of finding meaning and purpose in life and reduce one's risk of depression.
- Don't resist change because the status quo is familiar and feels safer. Failure to change negative attitudes, bad habits, and unrealistic expectations keep people stuck and miserable.
- The road to change begins with acknowledging sadness and fear. Mourn what is gone, then take small steps and risks to move forward.
- Create realistic goals.
- Others cannot define us without our cooperation.

We can accept or reject the stereotypes of older people. The power lies in each of us.

"I'm prescribing a laxative pill and a sleeping pill. Never, never take them together."

AN EASY PILL TO SWALLOW

I love my pharmacist. She does so much more than just fill prescriptions. She's my sounding board. She's my other medical go-to person. She makes sure I get what I need and need what I get. She has my medication blueprint right on her computer, which is great because it's easier to detect drug interactions and avoid potential life-threatening complications. When you consider most of us have prescriptions from different doctors and accumulate more medications as we age, having a relationship with your pharmacist can be a lifesaver.

I remember when I was on vacation and had a lousy reaction to a prescription drug. I was miserable. I was in tremendous pain. I called Mary. She was patient, informative, and solved the problem. Pharmacists are there in emergencies when your physician may not be available.

Another plus, your pharmacist will deal with the insurance company when necessary, which is enough to give anyone a migraine and another reason to take another pill.

Having a relationship with your pharmacist can also help with patient compliancy.

So, what steps can we take to make the relationship between patient and pharmacist more collaborative?

PHARMACIST MARY MCLAUGHLIN SAYS:

- DO USE ONLY ONE PHARMACY SO THE PHARMACY HAS A COMPLETE LIST OF MEDICATIONS.
- DO TELL YOUR PHARMACIST OF ANY DRUG OR FOOD ALLERGIES AND ANY PRIOR HEALTH ISSUES.
- DO TAKE YOUR MEDICATION EXACTLY AS IT IS PRESCRIBED BY YOUR DOCTOR.
- DO KEEP TRACK OF SIDE EFFECTS YOU ARE EXPERIENCING.
- DO KNOW WHAT YOUR MEDICATION IS USED FOR, DOSAGE, AND WHAT IT LOOKS LIKE.
- DO READ LABELS AND ASK QUESTIONS.
- DON'T TAKE ANY MEDICATION IF IT LOOKS DIFFERENT. CALL YOUR PHARMACIST IF IT DOES.
- DON'T TAKE ANYONE ELSE'S MEDICATION OR SHARE YOURS.
- DON'T COMBINE PRESCRIPTION MEDICATION WITH OVER-THE-COUNTER OR HERBAL OR VITAMIN SUPPLEMENTS UNLESS YOU CONSULT YOUR PHARMACIST.
- DON'T STOP YOUR MEDICATION OR CHANGE HOW MUCH YOU TAKE WITHOUT CONSULTING YOUR PHARMACIST OR DOCTOR.

IMAGE &
SELF-ESTEEM

Ever Notice The Older You Get The More You Look Like Your Birthday Cake?

AN ODE TO ME
by Dr. Ann Lane

Pendulous breasts
Cottage cheese butts
Crocodile skin
And a football gut.

Thinning manes
Droopy jowls
Spidery veins
And stubborn bowels.

Where is my beauty
Of not long ago
Where is my youth
Where did it go?

Essay No. 32

GENDER DIFFERENCES

MIRROR MIRROR ON THE WALL

The cruel reality of aging confronts us every day when we look in the mirror. When we pass our reflection walking down the street and notice that we are shorter, or have a profile that requires a second look, we might ask ourselves, "Who is that person?" For the fortunate among us who aren't affected by the aging process, I salute you.

But for the others, including myself, it's a constant battle between accepting, not accepting, and not having a choice—because it comes with the territory.

We survey our faces. We study our eyes and our crow's feet. We scan down to our marionette lines. To add insult to injury, what used to be a youthful, long neck now resembles elephant skin. And to think we complained about how we looked way back then.

Gone are the days when we see our reflection in the mirror and like what we see. Now, we sometimes get depressed. Or we see our mothers and even our fathers.

Men, whose once-chiseled bodies featured very proud six-packs, have softened with age. And while they may not be as verbal about their appearances, men think about how they look. They go to plastic surgeons to lift-up and fill-in. If you've ever watched the *Biggest Loser*, you see the raw honesty in the men, both young and old, as they struggle to lose weight, look like they once did, and feel accepted. There is no age limit on being judged.

Both men and women come to the table with their own set of social and cultural backgrounds. How they were raised, their experiences with their parents, and how they feel their parents perceived them.

I took my cue from my parents. Their opinion about my body was simple. I was too fat.   To this day, I carry that around. The biting remarks have dimmed with time, but in the background is this constant hum. My parents poured the foundation for how I would eventually feel about myself. Parents do that you know. They either accept their children and make them feel appreciated and that they can do no wrong. Or they fuel the flames of insecurity, where whatever their children wind up doing isn't good enough. As a young woman— well into my twenties—I tried Weight Watchers and really got thin. I finally liked what I saw in the mirror. I was certain I would make my parents proud. Their reaction: "Barbara, you're too thin."

It's a constant battle trying to strike a balance between how I feel about myself and what my parents thought of me.

The reality of getting older is reflective in so many ways. We don't feel older. It's our armor that is worn and rusting. Perhaps if society respected age a little bit more. Perhaps if Madison Avenue, the movie industry, and the publishing world were more inclusive of the broader audience when offering beauty, clothing, and fitness tips to women and men of an advanced age, we older people would feel more accepting of ourselves.

Is it any wonder why so many older people feel the challenges of aging and the need to keep up. It's very unsettling to feel invisible and less respected. Does this influence us when we look in the mirror? Hell, yes! Which begs the question: What is the reality of what we are seeing?

Take posing for a picture as an example. How often do we scrutinize ourselves in photos and not like what we see? And if we do happen to like what we see, we might need validation to make sure we are actually seeing what we hope we see. Remember that cameras, too, can distort. What about the angle? What about the lighting? What about the photographer? Do others see us the way we see ourselves? Do we see ourselves in the now?

We know our faces and bodies so well that it's become almost a daily routine to notice imperfections. But instead of seeing the entire self, we concentrate on bits and pieces of our whole self.

My bits and pieces were fixed during a couple of cosmetic procedures. I've had my eyes done and liposuction to reduce my saddle bags. I was supposed to have my neck done, but I had to give up two chins for two tits. I was diagnosed with breast cancer and chose to have a mastectomy. But I will get into that later. The point is: If you think it's broke, fix it!

"I can honestly say I love getting older. Then again, I never put my glasses on before looking in the mirror."
—Cherie Lunghi

Dr. Ann Lane says:

- Identify the things you like about yourself and list your strengths.
- Make a list of your life's accomplishments no matter how trivial you think they are.
- Do something new: Go back to school, paint, take up a hobby.
- Idealize values like loyalty, honesty, generosity, openness, good humor, empathy, and fairness. They set the bar for self-esteem.

The bottom line is: self-esteem is a work in progress.

Essay No. 33

THE ART OF DEFYING GRAVITY

You don't need to be an astronaut to defy gravity. You just need a good plastic surgeon. And having a wonderful aesthetician helps, too. And trust us, we have both.

Many years ago, when we were both broadcast journalists, we came to the realization that just being good reporters didn't cut it. We had to look good on camera as well. But that was becoming increasingly difficult. We knew that eventually we would have to do something about it—and the time was now.

Being in the business we were in, we fortunately knew who to call. We had every PR department in every hospital in our Rolodex (remember them?) and began the search for a magician to make us gorgeous.

Barbara broke the ice and had her eyes done. She says it's not so willy-nilly. There are protocols that have to be met. You need an EKG, blood test, and a whole battery of tests before they clear you for surgery. Then it was clear sailing. She chose to have the procedure done in the surgeon's own operating room. That morning, on an empty stomach, her daughter dropped her off. She ran in to get naked and put on a robe. She said: "Shoot me up with valium. Let's get started." It seemed to go very quickly and, once she peed, she was good to go.

It didn't stop at her eyes because, then, there were her thighs. Hello liposuction—goodbye saddle bags.

Carol, on the other hand, preferred the needle to the knife. She saw it done while she covered a news story on "Lunchtime Lifts" and it looked simple enough. Then she realized that watching someone get an injection of a dermal filler is easier than having the injection herself. Still, there's nothing like instant gratification. There were a couple of weeks of black and blue but, in the end, the years melted away.

Today, we still hit the filling station every couple of months.

If you plan on having cosmetic surgery, you have to do your research. We did a little of it for you.

DR. LYLE LEIPZIGER'S PLASTIC SURGERY TIP SHEET

- GET RECOMMENDATIONS FROM FRIENDS OR A FAMILY DOCTOR. YOU MAY ALSO BE ABLE TO FIND A QUALIFIED PLASTIC SURGEON IN YOUR AREA BY CONTACTING THE AMERICAN SOCIETY OF PLASTIC SURGEONS OR THE AMERICAN SOCIETY FOR AESTHETIC PLASTIC SURGERY.
- MAKE SURE THE PHYSICIAN IS CERTIFIED BY THE AMERICAN BOARD OF PLASTIC SURGERY AND AFFILIATED WITH A MAJOR TEACHING HOSPITAL. A BOARD-CERTIFIED PLASTIC SURGEON HAS COMPLETED EXTENSIVE TRAINING AND PASSED A SET OF RIGOROUS EXAMINATIONS.
- DON'T RELY SOLELY ON AN ADVERTISEMENT OR A PHYSICIAN'S WEBSITE WHEN CHOOSING A DOCTOR. ADVERTISEMENTS AND INFORMATION DISPLAYED ON THE INTERNET ARE NOT REGULATED. BE ESPECIALLY WARY OF ADVERTISEMENTS THAT TOUT COSMETIC PROCEDURES AT CUT-RATE PRICES.

PLASTIC SURGERY TIP SHEET (CONT.)

- Make sure any doctor doing a surgical procedure in his or her office has privileges to perform the same surgery in a hospital. You can call the hospital to find out. Ask if an operating room in a physician's office is accredited, which means it has undergone a comprehensive evaluation and meets the same high safety standards as a hospital operating room.

- Choose a doctor with whom you feel comfortable and who inspires confidence. Make sure the physician is willing to take the time to answer all of your questions in non-technical terms. The doctor should explain what you can expect in terms of the final outcome and recovery time. He should discuss possible risks as well as benefits.

- Ask the doctor how much experience he or she has in performing the procedure you are considering and ask to see before-and-after photos of previous patients.

- Make sure you understand all costs involved, including the fee for the surgery, anesthesia, the office-based operating room or hospital, and pre-operative tests. Cosmetic surgery is not covered by insurance.

- Have realistic expectations. Every patient is an individual, and while cosmetic surgery procedures can bring dramatic improvement, results can depend on age, skin elasticity, and other factors.

There are other things we think you should consider:

No one wants to see an older woman with overblown lips, so don't overfill.

If your eyelashes are getting as thin as the hair on your head, you may want to try a prescription for generic bimatoprost ophthalmic solution or use an over-the-counter product like Revitalash.

Even though Carol read that no one wants to see an old fart with a ponytail, she refuses to give hers up.

> *I've had so much plastic surgery, when I die they will donate my body to Tupperware.*
> —Joan Rivers

Essay No. 34

I-can-never-do-anything-with-my-hair-phobia

WHEN MY HAIR HAS TURNED TO SILVER
(A.K.A STEEL WOOL)

Ahhh…our crowning glories. As a teenager, I remember someone complimenting my "masses" of thick, wavy hair. Indeed, into my fifties, my hairdresser called me lucky to have such thick tresses. But I'm in my sixties now and—it pains me to say this—I can see my scalp. It's so pink and shiny. I hate it.

What happened to my thick, shiny hair? It used to be like silk. Now it's more pre-Raphaelite—wavy, dull, and thin. And like everything else pre-Raphaelite—dead. Our pesky hormones are doing yet another number on us—causing changes to the structure of our hair shafts. But it's not just that. If you happen to have long hair, the ends of your hair are probably a few years old and have suffered from sun damage, chemical dyes, and straightening agents, not to mention breakage from curling irons and just plain carelessness.

So, while our bodies may not be getting thinner, our hair is. Our follicles are producing narrower strands or stopping production entirely.

Our keratin is weaker and our melanin has abandoned us. Well, not entirely. You may find yourself more prone to age spots on your skin, but that's a different chapter. I'd never even heard of the phrase "female-pattern baldness" until recently, but that's what we experience once we pass sixty. And it's not just our lack of hormones. Hair loss could also be related to vitamin deficiencies or other health issues.

The woes surrounding our crowning glories are not limited to the texture, but to the color as well. In *The Aging of Hair*, researcher Ralph Trueb pointed out that by the age of fifty, 50 percent of the population is 50 percent gray. It's an easy statistic to remember and—I think it would be safe to say—keeps a lot of hair product companies and salons profitable.

Then there are free radicals (not to be confused with hippies coming of age in the 1960s). Free radicals help destroy our hair's cellular structure by making it coarse. The phrase "I can't do a thing with my hair" is now our daily mantra.

There are women who decide to allow their hair to go *au naturel* in their sixties. I've read articles in the *Huffington Post* and other news outlets about how freeing gray hair can be.

What else can you do? Hair transplants? Minoxidil? Biotin? Plumping hair products? Wigs? There are various remedies but none of them are perfect. One thing you can do is make sure you get your daily Recommended Daily Allowance (RDA) of iron, which carries oxygen to the hair, and zinc, which promotes growth, and B-complex vitamins, which help with shine and thickness.

EXPERTS SAY:

- DON'T WASH YOUR HAIR EVERY DAY. IT STRIPS THE OIL.
- USE A GENTLE SHAMPOO.
- LET YOUR HAIR AIR DRY.
- HAVE REGULAR TRIMS. OLDER HAIR IS MORE LIKELY TO SPLIT.
- HAVE A HEALTHY DIET OF FRUITS AND VEGETABLES, HIGH IN VITAMINS A AND C AND LOW-FAT PROTEINS.
- USE HAIR PRODUCTS WITH SUNSCREEN PROTECTION.

Unfortunately, as more and more of our scalp continues to show, we are just going to have to learn to grin and *bare* it. But wouldn't it be wonderful if we could pretend we are back in the 1930s and 1940s and wear a turban like Lana Turner in *The Postman Always Rings Twice?*

They're not gray hairs.
They're wisdom highlights.
—Author Unknown

"Sure it looks bad now, but try to imagine
it with the right shoes."

YOU WANT US TO WEAR WHAT?

There is something very endearing about watching young children play dress-up. Little girls wobbling around on high heels, their faces lost in a picture-frame hat, strands of white pearls draped around their necks. Their head held so high as if to say, "Look at me, Mommy, I am also a grown-up." And little boys wearing their fathers' suit jackets and ties while carrying attaché cases. They say this kind of play is toddler typical—age appropriate. Not so much with the seventy-five-year-old lady I saw leave the beauty parlor. It was a double-take moment. For anyone who has seen the movie *Grease*, Rizzo just left the building. Jet-black hair, teased, and sprayed to epic proportions. Tight ankle length white pants with her panty lines so very noticeable. Her blouse was see-through, too. Long dangly earrings and ridiculously high heels supplied the exclamation point. Maybe she was going for an audition?

Really, no matter our age, playing dress up doesn't end. Whether it's trying to look like a favorite movie star, model, or neighbor, we are constantly striving to achieve the "look." It just becomes more extensive, expensive, creative, and diverse.

We experiment with this, that, and the other thing. And even though we could hear a resounding NO in response to the outfit—like the lady leaving the beauty parlor—there is still more freedom to express your fashion self when you are younger. Here's the thing, when you reach a certain age—and look like you are trying too hard to look like you did *way back when*—opinions morph into judgments. Like the judgment I made regarding the lady in the beauty parlor.

Who doesn't want to look youthful? I sometimes feel nostalgic when I go shopping and try something on that, years ago, I would have considered fabulous on me. I try and recapture what I had. And what I had may not have been so bad. If only I had realized it then and appreciated it more.

But what exactly is "dressing your age?" It's a given. Today more women and men look fabulous in their sixties, seventies, and eighties. You would be hard-pressed to guess how old these people really are.

Even so, to achieve fabulousness, the first piece of advice I would offer is be comfortable in your own skin. That is foremost. Wearing confidence is always the best cover-up.

How often have you heard people say that older women should wear their hair short? For some that may be true, but it is not a one-size-fits-all rule. Look at Raquel Welsh and Jane Fonda. I wouldn't mind being older just to look like those incredible women. As a matter of fact, fashion rules hardly exist anymore, especially when it comes to color and wearing white in the winter.

I have heard fashionistas suggest to avoid selecting apparel that can be identified with a specific age group. One should opt for not too young or too old.

The bottom line: If you like what you see when you look in the mirror, go with it. Have fun and enjoy your day! Just try not to wind up looking like that lady in the beauty parlor.

EXPERTS SAY:

- MAKE SURE YOUR CLOTHING FITS PROPERLY. YOU WILL LOOK BETTER. MAKE YOUR TAILOR YOUR FRIEND.
- UNCOMFORTABLE CLOTHING CAN AFFECT YOUR MOOD.
- USE MAKEUP APPROPRIATELY. HEAVY BLACK LINER AND BRIGHT RED LIPSTICK ARE NOT FOR EVERYONE.
- YOU DON'T WANT TO LOOK YOUNGER. YOU WANT TO LOOK BETTER.
- JUST BECAUSE THEY SELL IT, OR YOU ARE GETTING A REALLY GOOD BARGAIN, DOESN'T MEAN YOU HAVE TO BUY IT.

The fashion magazines are suggesting that women wear clothes that are 'age appropriate.' For me that would be a shroud.
—Joan Rivers

OTHER STUFF

"You used to dial phones? Lick stamps?
Grandma, what are you talking about?"

GRANDPARENTS - A DAY TO PLAY

I loved my grandparents, especially my nanny, May. My grandfather was great, too, just quieter and less enthusiastic. They always made me feel special. They always made me feel that I was perfect without having to change one thing about myself. Nanny May was a pistol. I never heard my mother say, "Fuck." But my grandmother said it all the time. Thanks to her, I am bilingual. I not only speak English, but *cursive* as well. Maybe she learned it backstage. She told me she was a Ziegfeld Girl. She could have been because she was that beautiful. She had dark eyes, a beautifully sculpted nose, and full lips—tall with black, thick hair, and a nice figure. She was elegant.

My grandfather was just as handsome as my grandmother was beautiful. He was tall with thick white hair and a slender frame. They looked like they walked out of the pages of an F. Scott Fitzgerald novel. I used to love listening to my grandmother's stories. She told me that she once dated Al Jolson. Who knew for sure, but she was in that environment—so maybe. It didn't matter one way or the other. Her stories were thrilling. And I loved going on adventures with her. One holiday, I think Mother's Day, my mother, Nanny May, and I went to the St. Moritz Hotel in Manhattan for drinks. I was eight or nine at the time and Nanny May had one too many. She picked the cherry from her drink and stuck it up her nose! My grandmother always went for the laugh. Then she asked the waiter for another cherry so she could stick it up her other nostril. "Balance is good." We did crazy things together.

Interestingly, I never heard my mother tell my grandparents what not to do. I think my mother welcomed the involvement. When it came to boundaries, no one had them. As I got older and entered my teenage years, my relationship with my grandparents changed. I didn't see them very much and they felt bad. So, I made it a point to visit them at least once a week. I'd hear about the latest current events Nanny May quoted from *The National Enquirer*. As a matter of fact, she called me in college to report the latest medical findings.

My grandmother had a huge personality. She said what she wanted to say. She did what she wanted to do. It felt very liberating to be with her. She gave me the confidence to be who I am. She was downright outrageous and I adored her for it!

My relationship with my grandparents was special and uncomplicated. No ambivalence.

Grandparents come in all shapes and sizes with many different personalities. Whether they are serious, or off-the-wall funny and totally inappropriate, they are a gift!

The reason grandchildren and grandparents get along so well is that they have a common enemy.

—Sam Levenson

"I hope my grandma doesn't find out the
world doesn't revolve around me."

KEEPING THE GRAND IN GRANDPARENTING
by Dr. Ann Lane

As joyful and rewarding as grandparenting can be, it is not without its unique challenges. Circumstances, distance, and family relationships contribute to various role definitions. For example, there is the occasional visiting grandparent, or the one who's more involved in the care of the children. Your relationship with your children can also determine your role in their children's lives. While there are no hard and fast rules for varying grand parenting roles, there are a few guidelines that could be applied to most circumstances.

First and foremost, you need to decide what YOU want. How involved do you want to be? How much time do you want to spend with the kids? What responsibilities are you willing to take on?

Have a frank discussion with the new parents about their expectations. Their ideas may be very different from yours about how to grandparent. As kids go through different stages, expectations need to be reviewed.

If family tensions stand in the way of your relationship with grandkids, there may be residual issues with your own kids or conflicts with in-laws. Work them out! Parents are the gateway to the grandchildren.

Respect the authority of the parents. These are THEIR children. You may have different ideas about child-rearing but parenting is not your role. This is not your opportunity for a do-over.

Caveat: In extreme cases where there is child abuse or endangerment, rules change. There may be consequences for crossing boundaries, but the child's safety must always come first.

MAL-CONTENTS

"I AM NOT A PACK RAT.... I AM A COLLECTOR!"

LETTING GO

I remember watching a television show on which a woman couldn't bear to part with a box of trinkets that she said contained her dearest memories. A professional organizer explained to her that memories are kept in your heart and mind, not in a box. Tears followed, but the woman eventually came to terms with getting rid of most of what was cluttering her life.

Divesting ourselves of things we hold dear is difficult. When my father died, he left behind a houseful of stuff. It included a large shed crammed to the rafters with everything he and my mother had accumulated over a half-century. I think the reason was two-fold. First, my father grew up during the Depression. He had ten brothers and sisters, but his father had deserted the family and his mother died while he was still young. They didn't have much more than each other, and the older kids took care of the youngest ones. My father was second youngest. He grew up with very little, so he was reluctant to part with whatever he had. I think the second reason stems from the day my father cleaned out the attic and threw stuff away. He got rid of all the comic books my brother and I had saved over the years. We didn't know it happened until we saw a report on TV talking about how valuable some of the books had become. It mentioned a comic book my brother thought he owned. We ran up to the attic to find it and found an empty cupboard. We never let my father hear the end of it. I think that's what pushed him into becoming a hoarder.

After my father died, it was left to us to go through his possessions and decide what to do with them. He had a split-level house with an attic and a shed that was nearly as large as the house. Because he lived a few hundred miles away—and getting there took hours—cleaning out Dad's house became a project that took four years. My brother and I were amazed at what he had saved and how he stored it. We found worthless items that were well-protected and valuable items that were ruined because they had been placed in an uninsulated shed. I told my brother the story of the woman who said we carry our memories in our hearts and, after discussing each piece and what it meant to us, we laid it to rest in a dumpster. That experience gave us new memories.

Cleaning out Dad's house had a profound effect on me. It made it easier for me to get rid of things I had in my own home. I recently cleaned out a storage closet where I came across a pop-up book of ballerinas I remember getting at a book fair in the first grade. I cherished that book, but it was past its prime. So, I read it one last time before saying goodbye to the book forever. But that's okay. I now carry two memories of the book in my heart: One of the pleasure it gave me when I was little, and another of the satisfaction I felt in finally parting with it without feeling like a piece of my life was gone forever.

> *You spend the first part of your life collecting things… and the second half getting rid of them.* —Isabel Allende

DR. ANN LANE SAYS:

- PREPARE THE MATERIAL YOU WILL NEED SUCH AS BOXES, LARGE TRASH BAGS, FILES, CAMERAS, SCANNERS, AND SHREDDERS.
- CREATE CATEGORIES SUCH AS "KEEP," "THROW AWAY," AND "GIVE AWAY."
- BREAK THE TASK INTO TIME AND SPACE SEGMENTS TO AVOID FEELING OVERWHELMED.
- REWARD SMALL SUCCESSES (EACH COMPLETED STEP IS IMPORTANT AND COUNTS).
- ENLIST THE HELP OF A FRIEND OR FAMILY MEMBER FOR SUPPORT.

EXCERPT REPRINTED WITH PERMISSION FROM *HARFORD'S HEART* MAGAZINE

Consider talking to a professional to try to understand why you began hoarding in the first place.

TECH-NO!-LOGY

FROM IPHONE TO LIFE ALERT

They say you can't teach an old dog new tricks. And while some of you may take umbrage at being referred to as an "old dog," our learning skills can become more dulled with age. There is, however, more than meets the eye. According to an article in the British online media outfit, *The Telegraph*, older people appear to have more difficulty recalling facts because they have a lifetime worth of stored knowledge. The article compares a young person, who knows the birthdays of a few people and can recall them almost perfectly, with an older person, who may know hundreds of birthdays but has difficulty recalling them. Why? Because he or she has to sort through a lot more information. I don't know about you, but I find that kind of brain work exhausting.

The good news is that our ability to learn has not degenerated. We just take longer to process information because we are so knowledgeable. Do you hear that, you younger generations! Your elders are very, very knowledgeable.

What does this mean? It means that we sixty-plussers have no excuse for turning our noses up at smart phones and the Internet. We are just as capable of learning how to use them as anyone else. It's a funny thing the way the mind works. I used to struggle at the beginning of a new year when writing the new date on checks. Then I read in an article the reason why that happens. It's that we are afraid to let go of the old year. Since reading that article, I haven't had a problem writing the correct date. I hope this article is like that for you and technology. The next time you think, "I can't learn that," reprogram yourself to believe you have a great opportunity to learn something new. Maybe you'll be slower than those young whippersnappers, but that's because you already know so much more than they do. It just takes your brain a little longer to sort through your wealth of knowledge.

Of course, if you were never good at anything even slightly technical in your youth, you'll probably suck at it now. But don't blame it on your age. Each one of us has our own area of expertise.

When I first got a smartphone, I hated it. I used it for music and surfing the web but hated the idea of talking on it. It seemed to take so long to turn on, accept the call, and then turn on the speaker so I could hear the person on the other end. That is, until a friend said: "You know, you can just hold it up to your ear like a regular phone. You don't have to put it on speaker." I felt stupid, but then I thought about it. I am what the industry calls an "early adopter." I didn't have a whole school full of friends with the same phone, whom I could observe and mimic. I was an older adult and had no one to copy. Actually, I learned from a friend. And he learned from his son. You just don't immediately know how to use a product when you buy it. You have to read the instructions, experiment with it, and learn through trial and error. It may seem like it takes longer because it does. Our brains are like file folders stuffed to the gills because we can't throw out stuff. Everything's in there and staying in there. We sometimes forget information that we don't access too often. But when we are reminded, we say, "I knew that."

Someday, I may need a medical alert system—one of those buttons you wear around your neck that you press when you are in trouble.

All the owner has to do is pay the bill and press the button in an emergency—simple. But now that I accept that there is no excuse that prevents me from embracing technology, I can't help but think that I want something a little more sophisticated—like the ability to program it with music. Or ask it questions like an Amazon Echo or Siri. Or maybe I want an iWatch, so it's always there with me—a medical alert system that also tells me the time, weather, and monitors my heartbeat.

EXPERTS SAY:

- IF AT FIRST YOU DON'T SUCCEED, TRY, TRY AGAIN. PRACTICE MAKES PERFECT.
- ONCE YOU LEARN TO GOOGLE, YOU'LL NEVER LOOK BACK.
- YOU CAN FIND A WEALTH OF INFORMATION WITHOUT EVER LEAVING YOUR HOUSE. WHO NEEDS ENCYCLOPEDIAS?

Technology turns on a dime and advances like the wind. And while there will always be reliable ways to get help when we need it, we can't blame the way we receive that assistance on our lack of ability to learn new things.

INVESTED

WHEN YOUR NEST EGG ISN'T FULLY COOKED

My mother died when she was sixty-eight-years-old. I'm like her in many ways. So, my expectation—though I hope I'm wrong—is that I will die young. Anyway, I didn't think twice about leaving the workforce and taking early retirement to become a full-time novelist. But I digress.

Back in the 1990s, a Health and Retirement survey asked people over fifty if they thought they would live to be seventy-five. Now, more than two decades later, a recent Brookings Institute study reveals many people who answered that survey underestimated how long they would live, and that could have implications on their retirement savings. In the words of *Saturday Night Live's* Mr. Bill, "Oh nooooo!" According to the findings, half the people who didn't expect to be alive and kicking at seventy-five lived that long and more. Meanwhile three-quarters of the people who said they did expect to live past seventy-five—were right.

What does this mean to the majority of people over sixty?

Unless you have a sizable nest egg, you are in deep ca-ca. You could very well outlive your savings. I'd like to think that I'll win the lottery. But so far, it hasn't happened.

According to UBS Investments, a sixty-five-year-old couple is expected to amass as much as a quarter-million dollars in medical expenses throughout retirement. This is supported by an article that appeared in Forbes a few years ago, which predicted a retirement crisis in which millions of elderly Americans will grow to be "too frail to work, too poor to retire." It cited a statistic by independent experts that said as recently as 2010, 75 percent of Americans—that's three out of four people—had less than $30,000 in their retirement accounts. Can you spell D-I-S-A-S-T-E-R?

So, what can someone—who has already retired and no longer works—do to make ends meet?

ANNUITIZE: A single premium annuity provides a monthly check as long as the insurer stays in business. However, Senior Wealth Strategist Deborah Mamber advises that you stay with high-quality companies. "Anything that looks too good to be true probably is."

DOWNSIZE: Study your income and expenses and make cuts to your budget. According to Mamber: "Landscapers, professional house cleaners, etc. are often not necessary, especially for retirees. Local teenagers and neighbors can do the job, usually for lower prices and possibly even for barter. Babysitting, cooking/baking can be offered in exchange for cutting the grass and/or small repairs." You might also consider selling your home, some of your prized possessions, or a second car you rarely use.

ECONOMIZE: Rent out a spare room. Clip coupons. Take advantage of senior discounts. Get your books from a library instead of buying them at a bookstore. Consider a reverse mortgage. Work part-time if you are physically able. Call your city/town/village officials and find out what financial aid is available for the elderly. You may find help—from reduced taxes—to help with home heating costs.

RATIONALIZE: Running out of money should not equal catastrophe. Medicare, Medicaid, and Social Security should give you some help, but chances are you will have to change your lifestyle, possibly sell your home, and/or rely on the generosity of relatives. Even if you are not affected now, you may find yourself in a financial bind in the future. Just remember the old proverb, "Forewarned is forearmed," and make your financial decisions with the future in mind.

Tips from Investment Strategist Deborah Mamber:

- Keep an eye on your investments.
- If you are considering a reverse mortgage, you need to make sure about who the legal owner of the property is and if both owners are over the age required. There have been cases reported where one owner passes away and the other partner loses the house because he or she didn't understand all the ramifications of reverse mortgages.
- Your first move should be to cut out all the services you don't need. Landlines, premium cable, high-speed Internet, etc. Take advantage of bundle offers from various companies and see if they have special deals for seniors.
- In the winter, instead of heating the entire house at seventy-five degrees—especially if you tend to stay in one or two rooms—invest in an electric oil-filled radiator. It will keep a single room warm and you will save on oil/gas bills.
- Check out store brands of food. Very often they are made by the same companies as name brands but are sold at lower prices and go on sale more often.

And keep an eye on inflation. According to an article in *U.S. News and World Report*, most people "underestimate the impact inflation will have on their retirement plans."

"…. AND TO MY WIFE, ELIZABETH, WHO HATED MY GUTS, I LEAVE MY LARGE INTESTINE."

GOOD WILL HUNTING

I knew my husband and I needed a new will. We had been married for a long time and, through the years, our financial status changed. We had accumulated stuff and needed to protect our daughter and make it as easy for her as possible when we died.

It's certainly not a pleasant thought but being organized and knowing you are protected—and those you love are protected—certainly makes thinking about your day of departure a lot easier.

You don't have to be old or retired to have a will. As a matter of fact, we drew up our first will after our daughter was born to protect her if anything ever happened to us. Keep in mind, you don't have to be rich to have an estate. Any personal possession is considered part of an estate. If you own a car, home, bank account, furniture, bicycle—and want to bequeath any of these items to a special person—having a will guarantees your wishes will be carried out.

It's pretty unnerving to think you are going die. And knowing you need to make a will drives the nail in the coffin.

I try not to think about it. Robotically, I gather all the papers my attorney asked for and move forward. I feel more peaceful knowing that I'm taking control. But if you are in denial, and many people are, why don't you just think of it as making plans. Only don't put that on the calendar.

Our attorney helped us understand a wide range of issues: long-term care, how to protect our financial resources, how to minimize estate taxes, health care proxies, living trusts—and that's just for starters.

Attorney Stuart Schoenfeld says: "Getting proper counsel helps you make informed decisions. It's extremely important to make plans because not making a plan limits available options and allows others to dictate the outcome of these very important matters. If you don't say what you want, you may not be happy with what you get."

We knew it was time to take a financial physical and bare our assets.

ATTORNEY STUART SCHOENFELD SAYS TO TAKE THE FOLLOWING PAPERS TO YOUR INITIAL MEETING:

- ASSET INFORMATION: DEEDS TO YOUR HOUSE AND OTHER REAL ESTATE PROPERTY, BANK STATEMENTS, YOUR MOST RECENT IRS RETURN, YOUR HOME'S ESTIMATED VALUE, VEHICLE INFORMATION, AND EMPLOYMENT INFORMATION LIKE YOUR 401K, ETC.
- ALL CONTACT INFORMATION FOR THE EXECUTOR AND GUARDIAN OF YOUR WILL AS WELL AS BENEFICIARIES
- YOUR SOCIAL SECURITY NUMBERS
- MEDICAID AND/OR MEDICARE INFORMATION
- PREVIOUS WILLS
- LIFE INSURANCE POLICIES
- GIFT TAX RETURNS IF THERE WERE ANY
- ANY OUTSTANDING PAYMENTS DUE: MORTGAGE, LOANS, ETC.

ALSO KEEP IN MIND:

- IF YOU BECOME DISABLED BEFORE YOU DIE, YOU MAY WANT TO INCLUDE DETAILED INSTRUCTIONS FOR YOUR CARE.
- YOU CAN ALSO PREPLAN YOUR FUNERAL. THAT COULD PROVIDE A HUGE EMOTIONAL RELIEF FOR YOUR FAMILY.

Estate planning is for everyone. And it doesn't have to be expensive.

The only difference between death and tax is that death doesn't get worse every time Congress meets.
—Will Rogers

SOCIAL STUDIES

Essay No. 42

" It says here that you'd prefer someone with regular bowel movements..Does it matter if they're involuntary ? "

ARE YOU READY TO PUT OUT?

You would think that by the time your age creeps up into the sixties, seventies, eighties, and beyond, you might have accumulated more friends than you thought you would ever need. However, after the loss of a loved one, a move to a new home, or an incapacitation for one reason or another, you may find your social life in need of a booster shot. Dr. Ann Lane says: "Older men are reported to feel more isolated and lonely than women. But that appears to be more a function of marital status than any specific psychological factors. Women are better at forming relationships throughout their lives. They tend to rely on family and friends for emotional intimacy. Men tend to rely on their partners for emotional gratification and for connections to the outside world. Therefore, a single or widowed woman is less likely to feel socially isolated and lonely than a single or widowed man."

If you think about it, there are many ways to meet new people: dancing lessons, bereavement groups, volunteering, adult education courses like bridge, exercise classes, sports, and one of the more infamous ways— online dating.

You might be a little apprehensive taking that first step. After all, meeting new people requires that you talk about yourself and aspects of your life. In some instances, you might feel that your profile is incomplete.

Carol Scibelli, author of *Poor Widow Me*, says, "You're forced to look at your life because you're re-introducing yourself to strangers." She says that some people may experience fear, which could hold them back. According to *SucceedSocially.com*, you need to force yourself out of your daily routine and face the uncertainty. You also have to learn to be tolerant of rejection.

Think about your hobbies or favorite pastimes. If you like art, take an art class. If you like cooking, take a cooking class. These are just a couple examples of what you can do to meet people. They give you a chance to reintroduce yourself to society and learn something you have always wanted to learn.

Many people feel isolated and lonely. According to Lane: "Loneliness is often accompanied by depression, and depression often robs us of motivation and interest in others. Although e-mail, instant messaging, and social media can reduce the isolation and provide the human connections one so desperately needs, the emotional energy to do so may not be there."

If your feeling shy or scared, understand that you are not alone. There are other people in these groups who may feel the same way you do. If you feel socially awkward and don't know how you will be received by others, you may feel more comfortable if you are the one asking the questions. Ask people about themselves. Have they attended this group before? Where are they from? Ask simple, basic questions until the ice is broken.

Most importantly: Be yourself! Don't try to be somebody that you are not. Just remember how painful high school was. Being yourself will make you come across as more genuine. After all, you want to form relationships with people who respond to the real you—and not people who would only be impressed by a more trumped up version of yourself.

Like many things we do during our lifetime, taking the first step is usually the hardest.

THERE ARE A NUMBER OF SITES FOR MEETING NEW PEOPLE.

* *MEETUP.COM* WILL HELP YOU FIND PEOPLE WHO SHARE THE SAME INTERESTS YOU DO.
* *SUCCEEDSOCIALLY.COM*
* *SINGLESCRUISE.COM*
* LOOK ONLINE FOR "PAINT AND SIP WINE" PARTIES TO EXPLORE YOUR INNER ARTIST.

Take a deep breath, put one foot in front of the other, and enter the room. The only thing you have to lose is your loneliness.

My philosophy of dating is to just fart right away.
—Jenny McCarthy

"Everything takes grandpa a little longer to do. He's analog."

SLOW & CAN'T GO

Lately, it seems like I only have two speeds: Slow and Can't Go. It starts when I wake up in the morning. I was always a morning person who would jump out of bed at 5 a.m. Now, I lay there staring at the ceiling, then I sit at the edge of the mattress and stare at the floor. Finally, I stand up and wonder where I found the motivation to defy gravity. By the time I walk away from the bed, it's already nearing 9 a.m.

What happened to me? I used to be speedy, weaving in-and-out of slower pedestrians as I navigated the sidewalks of New York. I wanted to push everybody out of my way. They were slowing down my pace. Not anymore.

Back then, I never thought I would be the person slowing someone else down. I know growing older doesn't necessarily mean moving more slowly, but that's not the case with me. I feel like I need a lube job and a new pair of shock absorbers. Maybe that would put a bounce back in my step.

My driving isn't any better. But that might be because of being more responsible and fearing my mortality. Besides, who wants to pay another ticket? But I still get pissed when I'm behind someone driving slower than I want to go. I want to yell, "Get off the road, Grandma!" even though we might be the same age.

What's the rush? Where am I going? I'm a writer and work in my pajamas. So, I can take my time. It's a question of getting from room to room. I have all day to walk from my office to my kitchen. It's when I have to leave the house that it becomes a problem.

First there's putting on our face. For some of us, there's putting on our hair. And then the big decision comes when we are putting on our clothes: We have to decide what to wear.

But once we close the door behind us, we leave *Can't Go* behind and accelerate all the way up to *Slow*. It is what it is.

> *"My brain is like a cross between a colander and a lazy Susan— thin, slow, and it leaks."*
> —Ron White

RETIRED

Retired to most people means *I'm Done*. And feeling *done* may not leave us feeling so good. But if we put a different spin on the word and the actual day-to-day experience of being retired, we may be pleasantly surprised.

I am retired. It took me a while to get there because my identity was so wrapped up in my profession. It was who I was. And I was proud of who it let me be and feel. I ate, slept, and drank being a documentarian. However, there came a day when it wasn't doing it for me anymore, but I still held on because who would I be? I didn't want to just schlepp along, watch television, and eat Bon Bons. I couldn't let that happen. I needed to fill the void. I needed to continue to feel productive, have a sense of purpose, and feel valuable to myself. I wanted to look forward to the next day.

As unimaginable as it is to slam into olderhood, there is also a palpable sense of freedom. Strange, because this is in direct conflict with the anticipation of aging and all the stuff that goes with—what many refer to as—the third act. How crazy is that?

But I have learned if you look hard enough you can find a positive born out of a negative. If it works for a battery it can work for just about anything. And I was definitely feeling re-charged. But trying to get a handle on what I was actually feeling took time. And in time it came to me. I was feeling less irritated by people's expectations and social obligations.

A quote from Jean-Jacque Rousseau's came to mind. I heard it for the first time in a college philosophy class: "We are born free into a society of chains." Without delving deep into the mind of the man—and the real meaning behind the quote—it's an idea that always seemed spot-on to me.

We are obligated to abide by the rules and the law of the land. We may not like it but it keeps us safe. And it keeps order. But I'm talking about chain-bound obligations. Not to mention people with their own set of rules that they expect us to follow. They piss me off.

What age has given me is the freedom to unburden myself from bullshit.

YOU know how it is when you walk into your closet wanting to get rid of all the unnecessary stuff, but you just don't know if you should because you might wear it one day. After all, it's been hanging around for years. I say this: If it doesn't look right. If it doesn't fit right. If it doesn't feel right. Get rid of it! Bring your garbage to the curb. That includes people.

There are many different ways to feel free. And who says being productive is a one-size-fits-all.

It took time to get used to the "new." Change has always been difficult for me. I treaded through uncharted waters, looking for that special something. Then one day when I was pushing my shopping cart through the supermarket, I literally crashed into an old friend. I asked her what she was doing and she said, "Ballroom dancing." I tried it and discovered a whole new world.

I found my passion. It's exciting. It's challenging. And the challenges have brought me a renewed sense of ability and self-confidence.

And every time I hit the dance floor I know one thing is certain: I dance my way to happy!

Men do not quit playing because they grow old; they grow old because they quit playing.
—Oliver Wendell Holmes

WRITIREMENT

Ahhh...the golden years, a time when many of us choose to step away from our jobs (or be shoved out the door) and are faced with endless days—each one melting into another. For some people, there is still not enough time to get everything done. For others, boredom is the only way to describe their newfound excess of time.

I have often heard the phrase, "Everyone has a book in them," and believe it's true. If you have hours of precious time at your disposal, you have an opportunity to hunker down and write that book. We are not all Hemingway, but we don't have to be. Think of a caveman telling his story in the most rudimentary fashion—by carving, painting, and writing on the walls. It wasn't literature. It could have been a simple drawing of seven bison outside his encampment, six of them standing, the seventh lying on its side with a spear sticking out of it, and the caveman standing on top. But it tells a story—his story. History—we all have one. Why not make it easier to share with your family by writing it all down—your stories, happy and sad alike—whether they are your own or were told to you by other family members? Illustrate it with old photographs and identify everyone in the pictures with detailed captions. Nothing is worse than looking at old family photos and not knowing who anyone is. Include drawings and maps if it helps. Think of your life as a roadway between two cities. It's not a destination, but a journey.

This is not creative writing. It's not genre writing. You are not trying to write a best seller. You don't need to start with a line as memorable as "It was the best of times, it was the worst of times." You are simply journaling your past for the future. You don't have to be flowery or elegant. You just have to tell it like it was. If you have a natural gift for writing and can make the story more dramatic or entertaining without changing the facts, that's great. If not, that's fine, too. You only need to fulfill your role as family historian by writing down the major events that shaped your family during your lifetime. The simpler you make it, the easier it will be for others to read. Don't bore them with overly long histories. Stimulate them with straightforward prose that gets to the point. You want your family to appreciate your efforts rather than shoving the book under a bed.

THERE ARE MANY PRINT-ON-DEMAND (POD) PUBLISHERS WHERE YOU CAN HAVE YOUR HISTORY BOUND INTO A BOOK.

- BLURB (WWW.BLURB.COM) IS A GOOD ONE IF YOU HAVE A LOT OF IMAGES.
- CREATESPACE (WWW.CREATESPACE.COM) MAY BE THE ANSWER IF YOU HAVE A LOT OF TEXT.
- I'VE NEVER TRIED LULU, BUT I KNOW THAT'S ANOTHER POSSIBILITY.

Do a little research. If you need help, get a child or grandchild involved. It could result in starting a new tradition for your family—a tangible way of holding history in their hands—that they can pass on to the generations to come.

If Moses were alive today he'd come down from the mountain with the Ten Commandments and spend the next five years trying to get them published.
- Anonymous

DEAD END

SAVE THE DATE

I would imagine there are a number of you who have thought about your funeral. Thought about what your funeral would be like. Who will be there? Who will not be there? Who will be crying and who won't care? Will it be an obligatory I-have-to-go-funeral or one where the death is so tragic mourners can hardly breathe?

I have noticed through the years that people don't like talking about death, let alone talking about their funerals. Call it fear. Maybe not. Perhaps denial. Nonetheless, death has an extraordinary impact on our lives. So, going to a funeral to some is extremely difficult.

I don't know how I really feel about funerals. But I do understand the importance of the ritual.

Each of us shares a unique relationship with others, and attending a funeral gives us the opportunity to express and reflect upon what the deceased meant to us. It acknowledges the life of the person who passed, while helping us experience the reality of the death. For some, the ritual provides the opportunity to ask, "Why?" It helps many of us find meaning and deepens our understanding of our own existence. Most certainly we attend the ceremony so we can support the family with our presence. The ceremony gives us an opportunity to physically say goodbye. It helps us move past our own grief. It also gives estranged family members and friends a chance to catch up and eat out.

I don't know when I'm going to die, but one thing is certain, I don't want a long, drawn-out memorial about my life. If you are at my funeral you already know about my life, so why the repetition? I'm going to do my family, my grieving guests, and myself a favor. I am going to be prepared. I'm making out a guest list. If your name isn't on it, it means I wouldn't be caught dead with you.

Next on my "I'm-dead-to-do-wish-list" is planning what I'm going to wear. That's always been the exciting part of going somewhere. What I will be wearing and how I will look. I also want to be buried with my TV Guide and remote control. It's not going to do me any good, but it will drive my husband crazy. And when I am laid to rest in the coffin that I plan on picking out, please bury me with my dogs' ashes. The last time I checked, it was against the board of health regulations to be buried with your pets remains. Can you imagine that?

What may be a meaningful funeral to some may mean something entirely different to others. I do not want a doom-and-gloom funeral. Maybe I'll have my funeral at Long Island's Animal Game Farm. Or maybe the dance studio where I take ballroom lessons. It all depends on the weather. Contingency plans will be provided. I will have parting gifts for the mourners—loot bags like when we were kids leaving a birthday party. And I insist on no flowers. Such a waste. Make a donation to the charity of your choice.

Recently, I've noticed more funeral homes catering to lighthearted services. All you need to do is contact the funeral home of your choice, and the staff will help you preplan your funeral. Everyone benefits. It reduces the emotional stress on your family in making difficult decisions. It also reduces the likelihood of them making unnecessary purchases during an emotional time. What you want is what you will get down to the last detail. Funerals are expensive. Prepay to reduce rising costs.

FUNERAL DIRECTOR MICHAEL RESNICK SAYS:

- PREPLAN YOUR FUNERAL. IT REMOVES A LOT OF STRESS FROM FAMILY MEMBERS AND ENSURES YOU GET WHAT YOU WANT.
- TAILOR YOUR FUNERAL TO WHAT YOU LOVED IN LIFE. SOME PEOPLE HAVE SERVICES AT COUNTRY CLUBS, THE BEACH, THE ZOO, ETC.
- YOU CAN PLACE ANY ITEM IMPORTANT TO THE DECEASED IN THE COFFIN, AS LONG AS IT'S LEGAL.
- THERE ARE NO HARD AND FAST RULES. YOUR FUNERAL CAN BE WHATEVER YOU WANT.

It may not be easy thinking about your death, let alone preparing for your own funeral, but once it's all said and done, you can rest easy and get on with your life.

Being creamated..........my last hope for a smokin' hot body.
—Author Unknown

Essay No. 47

"As a matter of fact, you did catch us at a bad time."

EXCUSE ME!

So, the other day my husband told me he had a conversation with a friend who admitted to never wanting to get married again. On the other hand, my husband said he would. My heart sank. My ego was ripped to shreds. Here was a man that—if I died first—was supposed to mourn me till the day he died. I am the love of his life and, without question, irreplaceable.

He said: "You've got it all wrong. We have a good marriage, a great marriage. It's been a good experience, so why wouldn't I want to get married again?" I replied, "I wouldn't want to get married again." "Well," he answered, "I guess you aren't having as good an experience."

Trust me when I tell you, I have never felt more motivated to sell my jewelry!

MEMORY
LANE

REMEMBRANCE OF THINGS PAST

I remember…

- Phone booths.
- Flips, page boys, and beehives.
- When gas cost a quarter a gallon and you received a glass as a bonus.
- When Chiclets were five cents a pack.
- When bread cost thirty-two cents a loaf.
- The Army-McCarthy hearings.
- The Civil Rights Movement.
- When fashionable kitchens were harvest gold or avocado green.
- Kent State.
- When a slice of pizza and a coke cost a quarter.
- When you received a gift for opening a new bank account.

- When a subway token cost fifteen cents.

- When bus fare was ten cents.

- When a movie cost a $1.50 and a bag of popcorn cost a quarter.

- When cabs were twenty-five cents for the first quarter mile.

- When ties cost $1.49 at Tie City.

- Getting a steak, baked potato, and a slice of garlic bread at Tad's Steakhouse for $1.49.

- When beauty parlors charged $2.50 to style a woman's hair.

- Buying a new pair of Wrangler jeans for seven dollars.

- Wearing stockings before there were pantyhose.

- When "I had a dream in my Maidenform bra."

- When sanitary napkins came in gift-wrapped boxes and you had to use a belt to wear one.

- Voting for Miss Rheingold.

- A billboard at Times Square of a man smoking and actual smoke coming out of his mouth.

- Soupy Sales and White Fang.

- When TV couples could only sleep in twin beds.

- When gold cost thirty-five dollars an ounce.

- When parking meters were a nickel.

- Penny postcards and four-cent stamps.

- Brownie box cameras.

- When we didn't have area codes and phone numbers began with words.

- When a house in the suburbs cost $7,999 dollars.

- Elsie the Cow and the Campbell Soup Kids…"umm…umm… good."
- Air raids in school and having to duck under our desks with our heads down.
- Having to wear dog tags.
- Felt poodle skirts.
- Wearing galoshes.
- Playing girls basketball when you were allowed only two dribbles.
- Radio soap operas like Stella Dallas.
- Kate Smith singing God Bless America on her television show.
- Uncle Milty.
- No-Cal being the first diet soda.
- When TV dinners first hit the market.
- When Ayds was a diet candy.
- When JFK was shot.
- When Bobby Kennedy was shot.
- When Martin Luther King Jr. was shot.
- When Jimmy Hoffa disappeared.
- When the Challenger exploded.
- When Cadillacs had fins.
- When Chevy Corvairs were deemed "unsafe at any speed."
- Saddle shoes, white bucks, and Pat Boone.
- "I like Ike" buttons and "Click with Dick" clickers.
- When Doris Day and Rock Hudson were big at the Box Office.

- Jesus Christ Superstar and Tommy by the Who being the first popular rock operas.
- The MacGuire sisters, the Lennon sisters, and the Andrews sisters.
- Doing the "Twist" with Chubby Checker.
- When you didn't have to be politically correct.
- When there were no female news anchors.
- When the drinking age was eighteen and the voting age was twenty-one.
- When the UN moved to Manhattan.
- When the Empire State Building was the tallest building in the world.
- Horn & Hardart automats.
- Penny gumball machines and nickel candy bars.
- Ten-cent comic books.
- Hope & Crosby road movies.
- Martin & Lewis.
- Edgar Bergen and Mortimer Snerd.
- Ed Sullivan.
- Clem Kadiddlehopper.
- When you had to get up and walk to the TV to change the channel.
- Newsreels with Ed Herlihy.
- Cartoons before a double feature.
- Howdy Doody Time with Buffalo Bob, Clarabell, and Princess

Summer-Fall-Winter-Spring.

- Drawing on the TV screen with Winky Dink.

- When milk and seltzer were delivered to your door.

- "Plunk your magic twanger, Froggy" from Andy's Gang.

- Kukla, Fran and Ollie.

- Annette, Karen, and Cubby from the Mickey Mouse Club.

- Sergeant Preston of the Yukon and his horse Rex and dog Yukon King.

- Rocky and His Friends with Bullwinkle, Fractured Fairy Tales, Dudley Do-right, and Mr. Peabody and Sherman.

- Tugboat Annie, Beulah, and Hazel.

- I Remember Mama.

- Father Knows Best with Kitten, Bud, and Princess.

- Roy Rogers, Dale Evans, NellieBelle, and Gabby Hayes.

- The Little Rascals.

- The Paul Winchell-Jerry Mahoney Show.

- Ted Mack's Amateur Hour.

- The Edge of Night, Search for Tomorrow, and The Shadow.

- Quadraphonic and eight-track tapes.

- Victrolas.

- 78s, 45s, and 33 1/3 RPM records.

- When a computer took up an entire room and only NASA had one.

- Art Linkletter and People Are Funny.

- Queen for a Day.

- My Friend Irma.

- The Loretta Young Show.

- "My friend the witch doctor, he taught me what to say…"

- "Itsy bitsy, teeny weeny, yellow polka dot bikinis…"

- Rudy Kazooti.

- Go-go boots.

- Sleeping on rollers every night.

- Sputnik.

- "One Giant Step for Mankind!"

- When housewives in chiffon dresses, pearls, and high heels dusted with Pledge.

- When "the moon hits your eye like a big pizza pie."

- Mimeograph machines.

- When Ronald Regan was just an actor.

What do you remember?

OTHER
VOICES

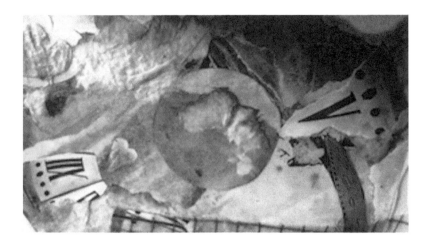

AGING
BY NORM SPIZZ

Adapting to a slower lifestyle.

Going to the bathroom four times each night.

Ignoring all the new aches and pains you never had before.

Not admitting that you can't do what you used to do many times.

Growing old gracefully.

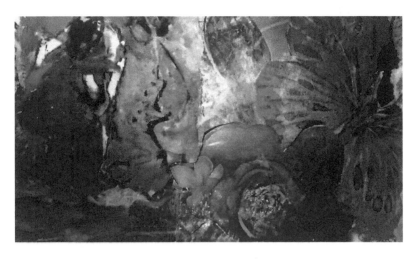

LIVING

BY JOAN BRITVAN

Living…
Going here and there, doing this and that.
Loving, holding, being held, being still.
Feeling with my hand and my heart.
Simply being…loving life. Engaging.
Always mindful of keeping the bounce in my step
And the twinkle in my eye.
Inhaling the spring air after a rainfall…breathing deeply.
Listening to the call of the red robin.
Holding grandchildren very close.
Sharing belly laughs, hugs, and intimacies
As well as tears to all those that deeply care.
Wanting it to go on FOREVER…
TIME:
Ethereal. Untouchable. Unrelenting. Unstoppable.
Those photographs—they hold back the moment.
Reflections. Freeze frame. Seizing the moment. Forever.
That's what I desire. To be in the moment. To seize the moment. To be
present. ALWAYS!

But now. Ah. Here's the wake-up call.   Here's the aha moment.
TIME.

It simply does not stop and like every well-told story there is, for us all…a beginning, a middle, and an end.

So, I will make my choice. I will stand in appreciation for all that I have had and all that is yet to come.

Being the best that I can be. With a bounce in my step and a twinkle in my eye!

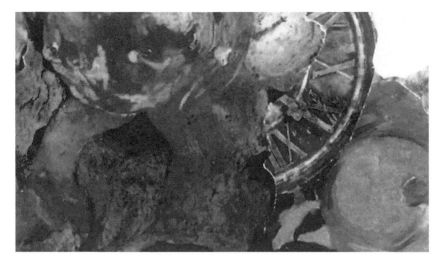

THE PHONE CALL
BY MICKEY BAYARD

Well, let's see: My prostate is gone. I have stents in my heart. My shoulder's been rebuilt. My sight is blurry. My wife passed. My pals are gone or going. And my memory? Shot.

But I must say, at seventy-one, I feel like a kid again. No kidding. How can I feel this way? Better still, why do I feel this way? At the risk of sounding like I'm writing a love song or smoking pot, I met a wonderful woman.

We first met in 2008. It didn't last. Two years prior, she had lost her husband of thirty-three years and wasn't ready to have a "meaningful" relationship. I was sad, but I understood. After all, it had taken me at least that long to adjust after my wife died.

Years passed and I often wondered how Carol was doing.

My daughters were twenty-five and twenty-three—and doing well on their own in New York—when I retired to Florida. I'm a golfer and my best friend was living there having a ball. Before I moved, I called

Carol on the pretense of just saying goodbye…or hello. I knew in my heart that I wanted her to know where I would be…just in case.

"C'mon over for dinner before you go," she said.

"What time?" I asked.

As I expected her to, she laughed. Her sense of humor was a big attraction for me.

"How about in an hour?" I said.

"But it's 9:30 in the morning," she replied.

"Pretend I work nights."

Best phone call I ever made.

Sorry. I digress.

Getting older is great. Getting old sucks!

I gotta run…it's time for our two-for-one colonic enemas.

So, I may be getting old but with Carol I am young again.

WALTZ WITH ME
BY FLO JACOBSON

I'm not one to use avoidance as a tool for coping, but upon reflection on aging, I realized that I don't want to think about the process. Every now and then, I hear this enormous knocking at my door and when I open it, I am flooded with the reality that I AM OLD! I know this because, when I hear that something happens to someone on the news who is many years younger than I am, they are referred to as elderly.

I try to shut it away. I don't think about it longer than moments, but it grabs me by the throat sometimes. My body parts are breaking down— deteriorating, wearing out—hip, knees, shoulder. Of course, gravity took over and changed the things that used to be "perky!" I don't want to dwell on this, so I don't.

I'm widowed, alone for many years. Life was not supposed to happen this way. My husband and I used to "practice" getting old. We would play at bickering, practice broken Yiddish, and shuffleboard to ready ourselves for retirement in a gated community in Florida. Life doesn't always happen the way we plan it...

What I missed most was passion, being held, being challenged in a way that brought me to a better understanding of myself. Accidentally, I found ballroom dancing. It is all-encompassing. Yes, it is the passion that I was looking for. It also creates the balance in my life that is selfishly mine. It keeps the demons away! Damaged body parts—who cares?

Creating new memories in a deteriorating brain...challenging at the very least. While I am on the dance floor, ask me how old I am? I am ageless! I am mind, body, spirit wrapped in a physical presence that feels only passion.

MY MEMORY
BY SHEILA TRONN TANNENBAUM

I have the worst memory.

I can't remember a thing.

Damn, where did I put my keys?

I can't remember what I came into this room for.

I can't believe I missed another date because I forgot.

My memory is the worst.

I have a terrible memory.

I don't believe this. Where did my memory go?

Forgot, forgot, forgot…it happens to everyone, starting much younger than "older" and yet we berate ourselves and make ourselves wrong every time. Damn me, I can't remember a thing!

We belittle ourselves and lament the (sometime) loss of our memory.

We punish ourselves for something that just can't be helped.

We are ashamed.

I say enough of that. Be kind to yourself instead of mean each time you have a forgetting moment. Decontextualize. Be gentle on yourself. The next time you are explaining a lapse to yourself or others say, "I have a soft memory."

Say it aloud now. Isn't it more a whisper than a shout? Doesn't it feel good?

Isn't it nice to be nice to yourself?

All it takes to have a soft memory is to say so. Soon it becomes a habit. It's a choice to have the inevitable side of memory loss be light rather than dark.

It's your choice.

Here's to your choosing to have a soft memory and enjoy your forgotten moments with ease, softly.

REGRETS & GRATITUDE
BY CAROL SCIBELLI

Unless I'm hit by a bus, choke on a chicken bone, or meet with another catastrophe, I'll be sixty-five tomorrow. Social Security and Medicare have been reminding me for months, sending annoying mail addressed to me, but obviously meant for my mother.

I guess I should be grateful that I made it this far and that my health insurance premiums will go down, but the odds are, so will my health. They say the sixties is a dangerous decade and, if you make it to seventy, you have a good shot to reach your eighties. But in what shape?

Is declining health and becoming feeble and dependent my fear? Well, it sure isn't my goal! In the old days, if I had a headache I took a Tylenol. Now, I assume I'm having a stroke.

Several years ago, I decided to buy Long-term Care Insurance. I almost changed my mind because the salesman's pitch was, "Do you want to live to be a burden on your children?" "Well," I said, "payback is pretty appealing." I twirled the pen in my hand.

In the end, I broke down and signed. Now my daughter and son are safe from changing my diapers. Since I'm a widow, though, I had to choose one of them to be my health care advocate. It was a tough choice. I had to look into their souls (and their bank accounts) to decide which one might be more motivated to pull the plug if I had the sniffles.

I recently heard that the Federal Government has an official term for those over sixty: "Elderly." That's right. "Elderly/over sixty." Evidently, I have been elderly for five years. This pretty much covers all my friends who, before this, I saw as fun and vibrant—even though, I admit, it's tricky for most of us to stand from a sitting position.

I've lost many of my loved ones over the years: both of my parents, my sister, my husband, and most recently my favorite nephew. Except for my mother, all of them were in their fifties and it's awful to grasp that they will never evolve to be more of who they might have been.

As much as it's painful to be left here missing them, it's also a blessing. I get to know my grandkids. I get to see the world bloom with technology that I never could have imagined and often can't figure out.

All their lives, I told my children that we regret the things we don't do more than the things we do do. (When they were young they giggled at do-do.) I look back and wonder with some angst if I made the right choices at key moments. What were the opportunities that I let slip by that may have led to something wonderful?

My contemporaries are baby boomers who are retiring and I feel like I'm still the kid who was told in high school, "Carol is not living up to her potential." Maybe I was. Or could it be that I did underachieve and waste years. Do I have more to contribute? Is there time?

That was wearing on me until just now. My ninety-one-year-old friend,

Shirley, who drives, dances, and swims, and knows more about world events than I do, called and said, "Carol, I'm beginning to slow down, but my children are in denial. I told them, 'You know, kids, I'm not sixty-five anymore.'"

MUSINGS OF A 70 PLUSSER
BY ANN LANE

As I write about this phase of life, I find myself bristling at the use of descriptives available to me: senior, elderly, aged, older citizen! Being seventy-plus myself, I cannot identify with any of those adjectives. None of the people I know or work with fit the image those words conjure up. Even the current commonly used term "boomers" only brings to mind a drooling, ambling, overenthusiastic hound. I still have not found more appropriate terminology but "New Age Adult" has a nice ring.

THE WOW OF NOW
BY RABBI LYNNDA TARGAN

I recently read a sign that blared, "The older I get the better I was." Oy, not the most optimistic endorsement of aging. But it sure got me thinking...

It's true, my figure used to be leaner, my face less lined and saggy, and my memory crackerjack. Fortunately, I learned early on that it isn't those external manifestations that are sustaining over the long haul. The key to a happier life is attitude and engagement.

During my mid-fortieas, after a successful career in public relations, I engineered a life-changing transition, which resulted in my becoming ordained as a rabbi at age fifty-five. Accomplishing the goal at mid-life opened up a new path of opportunity for me at a time when many people my age were slowing down, retiring, or disengaging. It solidified my relationship with God and fortified my strong connection to the beautiful rituals of Judaism, Israel, and the Jewish people, which I find more and more compelling as I mature. My new work affords me the satisfying opportunity to be a capable teacher and puts me in a unique position to be helpful to individuals and groups during their pivotal times of triumphs and tragedies.

Now at sixty-seven, I remain busy and connected, and compared to many women of my baby-boomer generation who complain about feeling irrelevant, invisible, and outside the cosmic conversation, I'm plowing ahead full throttle. The shift began in earnest when I made a mindful choice and set an intention to live my days filled with beauty, meaning, and purpose. And that approach has been the counterpoint to the necessary losses we must all sustain if we are privileged to enjoy advanced years. But maintaining physical and spiritual health as we age is a work in progress and an ongoing process.

Whether it's walking through a new neighborhood in a local city, watching the waves roll back and forth on the coastline, or biking through a rolling green countryside, the WOWs are ubiquitous and beg to be noticed and savored. Especially during the aging process, it's up to each of us to find and identify our own WOWs and to feel blessed in their appearance. Creating sacred space to receive the WOWs is about balancing the busyness with silence and stillness, and for me that has made all the difference.

Yes, in some measure, "The older I get the better I was." But without this life-extension, I wouldn't have been the recipient of many treasured gifts, which people like my mother, who died at age forty-nine, had been deprived. I wouldn't have felt the love of a wonderful husband for almost five decades. I wouldn't have seen my children become independent and flourish in their own right. I wouldn't have experienced the sheer bliss of two grandchildren or generated cherished memories with my beloved extended family and fantastic friends. So, on balance, I'm finding olderhood a very decent place to dwell.

TENNIS, ETC.
BY FRED LANE

Sometimes I fantasize about having time with nothing to do but rest. But my days and weeks are filled with tennis, caring for our dogs, TENNIS, working with my wife on our charity, grandkid duties, TENNIS, keeping in touch with family and friends via e-mails and texts, TENNIS, dates with my beautiful seventy-one-years-young wife, sampling new restaurants, exercise, TENNIS, occasionally going to or watching a game, reading, TENNIS. Oh well, I guess someday I will rest but not now, not yet. I'm not ready!

"*He was a great writer.*"

OUR SINCERE APPRECIATION TO ALL THE WONDERFUL PROFESSIONALS WHO HELPED WITH
Over-Sixty: Shades of Gray

Elliot L. Auerbach, D.D.S., P.C.
Periodontology & Implantology

Clifford M. Berck, M.D.
Dermatologist

Wendy Fried, M.D., FACOG, F.A.C.S.
Northern Obstetrics & Gynecology

Jerry Gold, Ph.D. ABPP
Clinical Psychologist

Leslie P. Goldberg, M.D.
Long Island Eye Surgeons

Melanie Herzfeld, Au.D.
The Hearing and Tinnitus Center

Karen Kostroff, M.D., F.A.C.S
Chief of Breast Surgery, Northwell Health

Jessica Kreshover, M.D.
Urologist

Ann Lane, Psy.D.
Clinical Psychologist

Lyle Leipziger, M.D., F.A.C.S.
Chief of Div. of Plastic Surgery, Northwell Health

Deborah M. Mamber
Senior Wealth Strategy Assoc., Empire Group

Mary McLaughlin, R.Ph.
Pharmacist

Michael Resnick
Sinai Chapels

Stacey E. Rosen, MD, FACC, FACP, FASE
Cardiologist, North Shore - Northwell Health

Marni Schefter, R.D.
Registered Dietician

Stuart H. Schoenfeld, Esq.
Elder Law

BARBARA'S ACKNOWLEDGEMENTS

Where would we be today without the help, encouragement, intelligence, patience, generosity, cooperation, and friendship from the following:

To my loving husband, Michael, who is one of the most decent, honest guys on this planet—my rock who has supported every path I chose. But the question still remains—after almost fifty years of marriage— who gets the medal?

To my daughter, Jennifer. Words cannot describe the love, devotion, and admiration I have for you. The biggest gift in my life was given to me the day you were born. You are my breath.

To my best friend, my chosen sister, Dr. Ann Lane, who always gave me the love, respect, and support to make me realize, I'm worth it. Who always had my back and knew me better than I knew myself. Who pulled me up when I was down and gave me the courage to face myself.

To my shrink, Dr. Jerold Gold. Your couch has been one of the most comfortable couches I have ever sat on for oh, so many years. Thank you for all your wisdom. Thank you for all your insights. Thank you for having an office only twelve minutes away.

To all our friends who took the time to share how they feel about aging. Their testaments underscore what we already know to be true— we can still kick ass no matter how old we are!

What would we do without you Dr. Ann Lane, Fred Lane, Carol Scibelli, Norm Spizz, Mickey Bayard, Flo Jacobson, Sheila Tronn Tannenbaum, Rabbi Lynda Targan.

And to my very talented college friend, Joan Orlinsky Britvan, who by the way is still as gorgeous as ever, thank you so much for your gorgeous art work, which we used for "Other Voices."

202 Barbara Paskoff & Carol Pack

To Fred Lane: Thank you for being the bright light in all our lives. We miss you!

To Dr. Joseph Gymesi, my first shrink, who encouraged me to write and who promised me he would never die. Well, that didn't work out so well. You will always have a place in my heart.

Our thanks to agent, Grace Freedson, who passed up representing us, but was kind enough to nudge us in the right direction.

You never know when a query rejection we responded to would develop into a friendship. E-mail after e-mail to let's get together and have a drink. Our thanks to June Clark for the invaluable help she gave us with re-writing and re-writing and re-writing our proposal.

To our very dear friend Carol Scibelli. You are smart, clever, and witty and we wanted you to write this book with us. But you said NO. We missed you.

Henry Ford said: "Coming together is a beginning. Keeping together is progress. Working together is success." And it was just that, thanks to my co-writer and friend whose extraordinary talent, creativity, and incredible command of the English language have made this journey one of the most rewarding, challenging, and exciting experiences one can ever hope to have.

Carol and I believe we have created a very unique, entertaining, and informative book. We hope you agree.

Time for drinks! Enjoy!

CAROL'S ACKNOWLEDGMENTS

This book would not be possible without acknowledging the support of several people. First and foremost, my devoted husband Andrew, who picked up the slack and suffered in silence—mostly—while I remained locked away in my office working on this book.

To my brother, Carl, and sister-in-law, Maureen, who have always encouraged me and patiently listened to me drone on about my writing projects. And a loving nod to my three nephews who always manage to entertain me.

To my "twin-separated-at-birth" cousin, Joann, who gave me supportive feedback during our almost daily e-mails and who has been my sounding board for everything having to do with aging. And a sincere thank you to all the rest of my family who have never pelted me with rotten tomatoes, which I consider a positive sign.

My sincere thanks to Carol Scibelli, who is always an inspiration and contributed to this book (although not as much as we would have liked). And to Ken Eckhardt and Chris Hendriks, who listened to me nattering on about the writing process over our sporadic lunches, yet still remained supportive (although it might have been they were just enjoying their food).

Thanks to June, Grace, and even the agents who didn't want to change their letter of agreement for us, for all the valuable feedback they gave us. And a special thank you to our editor Nick Nigro, who we may have possibly driven crazy, but who still responds to our emails.

A SUPER-BIG hug to my co-writer, Barbara, for her commitment to this project. Her circle of friends and professional connections are a tremendous asset, and their endorsements and encouragement kept us buoyed when it felt like we were sinking. Barbara is a go-getter. I'm a rock (and only move as often). As writing partners, we are yin and yang. Together we have created something that we hope will keep friends and strangers alike informed and entertained.

ABOUT THE AUTHORS

Barbara Tuerkheimer Paskoff, a founding partner of Envision Productions, Inc., and a former broadcast journalist, has produced and written medical and public affairs programs since 1988 for PBS and cable stations. Her work has been broadcast throughout the United States. She has received four Emmy nominations, as well as awards from the Press Club of Long Island, New York State Broadcasters Association, Long Island Coalition for Fair Broadcasting, the Aurora Award, The Columbus International Film & Video Festival Award, The American Medical Association International Health and Medical Film Competition Award, and the New York Institute of Technology Alumni Recognition Award. She has written, produced and directed medical education videos for pharmaceuticals, doctors, and patients. She has also served as Executive Vice President of the Society of Professional Journalists—Long Island Chapter. She divides her time between writing and competitive dancing. She received her BS from Emerson College in Boston and her MA from New York Institute of Technology. Born in New York, she now resides on Long Island with her husband, Michael, and two fun-loving rescue dogs.

On a personal note, in 2008 I was diagnosed with breast cancer. After the rigors of a mastectomy and chemo I knew I needed to get out of my head. I had to stop looking back and begin looking forward. And so I began ballroom dancing at the age of sixty-four. Whoever would have thought at seventy-three I would still be going full steam ahead, traveling to different venues to compete. Dancing makes me feel alive. It gives me a sense of purpose; it challenges me. Dancing gives me balance, not to mention a better figure and stamina. I have learned that mountains are to be climbed, not to walk away from. And once you get to the top of the mountain, whatever your mountain may be, there is an incredible feeling of accomplishment.

ABOUT THE AUTHORS

Carol Pack is an award-winning former journalist, news anchor, assignment manager, college professor, and a former president of the Society of Professional Journalists—Long Island Chapter. During her journalism career, she taught more than a thousand graduate and undergraduate *NYIT* college students how to get jobs as broadcast journalists at its internship, *LI News Tonight,* and she considers herself the fairy godmother of news reporters around the world. She also worked as a news writer for WNBC-TV, News 12 Long Island, and GNYC News. She has received numerous awards from various media organizations including the Press Club of Long Island, Fair Media Council, New York State Broadcasters Association, and the Society of Professional Journalists. In 2018, Carol was inducted into the Long Island Journalism Hall of Fame.

She now has a second career as both a non-fiction author and a novelist, and Carol has just completed a trilogy within her young adult fantasy series known as the Library of Illumination. *Kirkus Reviews* named *Chronicles: The Library of Illumination* one of the best books of 2014 and has given a critical nod to each of the subsequent books. She is also the author of the historical fantasy series: *Evangeline's Ghost* and is currently working on *Evangeline's Ghost: The Bridge.*

Carol received both her BA and MA from New York Institute of Technology. A native New Yorker, she lives on Long Island with her husband Andrew and a picky parrot.